The Green Book:

Caring for Each Other Sustainably

– BOB RHODES –

An environmentally friendly book printed and bound in England by
www.printondemand-worldwide.com

This book is made entirely of chain-of-custody materials

If life is a struggle to achieve, then in its shadow is the struggle to remember what is worth achieving. The welfare state is one of the great modern achievements, but today we wonder what we've lost by our own thoughtlessness and ambition. We cannot go backwards; we don't want heartless cuts and increased prejudice. But it is time to rethink the design of the welfare state. At its heart should not be public services but active citizenship, friends, family and community. We need a welfare state that combines justice with citizenship. Resources like The Green Book offer us hope. They remind us that we can still reflect, rethink and build anew - and enjoy the journey to justice together.

- Dr Simon Duffy, Director of The Centre for Welfare Reform

www.fast-print.net/store.php

The Green Book: Caring for Each Other Sustainably

A catalogue record for this book is available from the British Library

ISBN 978-178035-603-7

First published 2013 by
FASTPRINT PUBLISHING
Peterborough, England.

To:
Daphne, Dan and Amy Marie

WELCOME TO MY TAKE ON AN ABSURD WORLD!

It seems to me that the various societies that people the earth are ordered by powers that are sometimes obviously but in most cases invisibly controlling things. Generally their superordinate authority is masked by a confusion of competing claims for citizen's commitment which are sometimes tribal or nationalistic, often religious, or, rarely these days, truly political. However, with few exceptions, these causes implicitly acknowledge and serve a greater power – the power of money and of those who wield it. The power of those who – and this may be a simple explanation of globalisation – insist that all life can be described through the prism of financial transactions; the market.

And that worries me; not owing to any superior or occult knowledge on my part or any dogmatic certainty. In fact it is my own uncertainties and awareness of the abstractions, inconsistencies and ambivalences that inhabit my limited understanding of my own experiences that cause me to be so untrusting of those who express certainties when, from my perspective, they seem to be so wilfully disregarding obvious dilemmas that are likely to attend upon their prescriptions.

It seems to me that - for all the perceived benefits of mass miscommunications, the intermarket, the asocial media, 24 hour TV 'stories', and all the other sit on your backside and consume it paraphernalia that many assert cause us to be better informed and connected – we might, as a society, be subject to more successful grooming, marketing and subversion by a relatively smaller and more powerful ruling elite than has been manifest ever before in human history?

And I worry that it is possible that we are sleepwalking into a future where more and more of our fellows will be sacrificed for the short-term interests of the controlling few.

It seems to me that a globalised and marketized hegemony will never grasp and maturely address the fundamental issues upon which the future of humankind (not the planet!) truly depends. As long as profit rules, greed induced global warming, poverty fuelled over-population, child-killing environmental diseases, malnutrition and starvation arising from non-attendance to locally sustainable food production, the proliferation of weapons of all kinds and hence wars and so many other sustainability and survival challenges will fester.

It seems to me that, if energy security was simply a matter for local people, few if any would choose the on their doorstep nuclear power station or short-term imported gas 'solutions' over the sustainable wind and tide alternatives that they so naively demonise.

Having spent a working life engaged in what is now, quite appropriately, generally referred to as the care industry I have taken to thinking a lot about how we care for and, as often as not, fail those whose love for us deserves our care. In one career I have been witness to vocation being redefined as business, to citizens with rights and responsibilities reconfigured as consumers, to the families to which all of us (who stand a good chance some day of needing some help) belong being relegated to the role of supplicant customers, and of those communities to which most of us have contributed so much being defamed as potentially exploitative and abusive of us when the system decides that we should be categorised as vulnerable. And it seems to me that the absurdity that I perceive in my world of monetized 'care' is an illuminating allegory of the wider world of monetized life. In *Much More to Life than Services* I made a plea for our service institutions to recognise their limitations and the usually unintended dire consequences of setting out to do things that can only be realised through love and relationships. It is counter-intuitive to ask professionals and institutions to step back a little and restore power and responsibility to their 'customers' and hence the source of their power and wealth (livings). But lots of individuals do understand and aspire to respond to their dilemma. Their struggle is inevitably strengthened when the people and communities they serve come to a sharing of their insight.

So, in *The Green Book* I have set out to do something which is an even tougher 'ask'. I have set out, with a number of contributions from my LivesthroughFriends friend and co-conspirator, Colin Campbell, plus a few nuggets from other thinkers, to put together a cross between a coffee table 'dipper', a common-place book and a contemporary *memoriam mortis* that is nothing more or less than an inducement to think deeply, reflectively, creatively or subversively and, if the mood takes you, vengefully or angrily about our society, our relationships, our responsibilities, our expectations for ourselves, and the world we will pass on to our children and inheritors.

This is a book of true stories, poetry, parodies, songs, quotes, reflections and ideas. The passions and sentiments are those of the writers who have set out not to convert or apostatise but rather to stimulate independent, free and unfettered thought. Hence I am setting out to do something truly counter-cultural in this modern world of instant response and gratification. Instead of subtly, or indeed blatantly, telling you the reader what to think, and then piling on the evidence – an old colleague used to say, "Bullshit baffles brains", and showed a rare insight – we're simply going to share experiences, ideas and perceptions, acknowledge the limitations of our own conclusions, and leave the interpretation and thinking up to you. Because, it seems to me, folk who are thinking, and regularly revisiting and iterating their interpretations, are far less likely to become distracted and diverted sleepwalkers who follow the crowd to...; you decide. I hope you find what follows thought provoking and occasionally entertaining.

Bob Rhodes February 2013.

BRIDGING THE RUBICON: "ALL ABOUT SERVICES"

A few days ago I met some inspiring people who had succeeded in the eye-watering commission of brokering a regional five year "Strategy for Adults with a Learning Disability" between 5 local authorities and a health board. I was flattered. They met me to explore whether I would consider chairing the key implementation mechanism for the strategy, entitled *Meaningful Lives*. I had been advised in advance that critical friendship and radical thinking would be central to the contribution I might make, and that my stance might be "a bit rich" for some tastes. I'm relieved to report that I connected happily and easily with all my hosts but not, it transpired, with the Strategy document which I took away to read after the meeting; a document that bears little relation to the exciting and optimistic conversation I'd enjoyed with its proponents.

I should not be surprised at people's capacity to tolerate and disregard intellectual dissonance, illogic and contradictions. After all I've spent most of my 'leadership' life addressing institutionalisation, socialisation, and organisational change. But I always am.

To kick off our discussions I'd asked for a summary of the vision and how it had been evolved. There was joy on the face of my informant when he described how the Strategy had its roots in consultation with "service users and carers" and that the key priorities specified and developed in the plan fully reflected their wishes. I observed that, historically, such consultations have too often been pre-empted by the programmes and services flavour of the questions asked and constrained by the limited knowledge and experience plus institutionalisation of the respondents. These observations were taken on board – which I found really encouraging given my day by day experience of defensiveness and rationalisations – and led to vigorous discussion of what has been learned from asking open ‘Good Life’ or “what really matters and is essential to you leading the life you want despite your frailty or disability” questions. I had pointed out that, while it was reassuring that some people had identified a desire for friendships and relationships as top priority (it came top with 42 votes out of 246 cast so was only important to a sixth of respondents in the context of this exercise), nearly all of the priorities were recorded in language that related to services. This was hardly surprising as, when I got around to reading the document, it stated that participants had been “asked to identify the key themes and priorities for learning disability services”. Subsequently, it seems, the same exercises had been undertaken with a full cross-section of institutional stakeholders and the priorities forthcoming checked against the “national legislative and policy framework and related local health and social services strategies”. The document does not tell us how things might proceed if peoples’ wishes did not comply with pre-ordained constraints.

With hindsight the dissonance between our on-going conversation and the strategy document is all the more bizarre. I had developed the conversation by suggesting that the role of services should be supplementary and complementary to, and sustaining of, lives based upon relationships and belonging (that is, for the avoidance of doubt, lives spent reciprocally and interdependently amongst family, friends, neighbours and the communities within which folk contribute and associate). We’d talked enthusiastically together about the potentials inherent in self-direction, about the leadership challenges associated with reversing the current of social care consumerism and dependency, of educating the wider political and bureaucratic cultures away from fixing and social engineering to enabling and supporting, and been excited by the possibilities engendered by restoring and supporting civil society and returning power and responsibility in that context to citizens. We’d been in clear agreement that the starting point lay in helping folk get clear about what matters most them and then helping them generate lots of possible routes to evolving the outcomes that make their lives progressive and fulfilling. We'd animated discussion about methods for promoting effective and creative thinking both in the workforce and amongst the wider population. We'd told stories of creative solutions and the evolving nature of real lives as against the episodic and often inert realities of service interventions. Without doubt we had 'buzzed'.

So it was disappointing, on reading the strategy, to see the same old chestnuts, the service and institution centred assumptions dominating the core principles that were deemed to have been derived from consultation with citizens. Instead of statements starting with terms such as People, Citizens, Families, Networks, Circles, Associations, Peer(s), Communities and Neighbourhoods the emphasis of nearly all of the thirteen statements stated or heavily implied, "Services should". On not one occasion did a statement lodge the power nor the responsibility with individuals or families. And the killer statement - that sums up the worm in the bowels of the thinking and places all accountability and authority squarely in the hands of local authorities and professionals, and which paradoxically follows immediately after the injunction to "promote independence and social inclusion" – is set out in principle 2:

❖ *A* ***comprehensive*** *range of* ***services*** *should be available for people with a learning disability which* ***provide timely****, responsive person centred* ***solutions"*** *(my emboldening)*

Any objective examination of the document will leave the reader in no doubt about the implicit beliefs, assumptions and, perhaps unwitting and unintentional, objectives of the authors. Implicitly the most important element of the lives of people with learning disabilities is, in this institutional culture, the public services that they receive. There is barely a hint in the document of any other perspective. As a consequence the whole tenor of the strategy is concerned with service improvement and user and carer involvement in their oversight.

When a Carer explains that, "Carers need emotional, practical and social support", the Strategy immediately asserts that, "it is necessary to ensure individuals have access to appropriate information, a carer assessment and a flexible and creative range of support options to meet their respite needs. In addition carers should have opportunities to access appropriate training and support." In other words serviceland is saying, "We've got the answers. Just plug into our comprehensive services. It's just a matter of funding them." And that, frankly, is plain stupid! Carers who have, or have been helped to have, their own meaningful lives with intentional and loving (hardly a service term!) networks of family, friends, neighbours and enabling professionals deem the service options, when available, as hollow alternatives. And, beyond that, when I have something to sort out I habitually ask myself how might I or we (preferably) *possibly* deal with this. I doubt that if I need emotional, practical or social support that public services will figure high on my list of desirable possibilities.

And so, if I do have the opportunity to assist these authorities along the journey to enable people with learning disabilities in this part of the world to secure and sustain meaningful lives, the first thorny question will be how we might reinvent the strategy so that it reflects and reinforces the aspirations and passions of the people I met. I guess that a good starting point will be to develop a concise and simple guide to the strategy that will become the implementation 'bible'? This should provide clarity of vision – clear about values, beliefs and principles; clear about required outcomes; clear about the subsidiarity of 'serviceland; and, crucially, setting out the initial targets for systemic and behavioural change – asking and responding creatively to the 'good life' question would seem to be the most apt launch pad. Additionally, in setting out a vision for how the 'social contract' between citizens and their public services will be rekiltered, the 'agenda for action' document needs to be explicit that everyone is part of this transformation and that, at the least, representatives of everybody will be actively engaged in its iteration.

In closing I make a very simple observation. When we set out to bring about change and this a validated by a public statement that takes its credibility from its roots in the democratic process and public consultation it is crucial that we design and carry out the consultation exercise with reform rather than tinkering in mind. This consultation implicitly announced that the intention was to fine tune and improve the existing machinery rather than explore more effective possibilities. Now it will be necessary to do the consultation again as part of the implementation of a reform strategy. It would be sensible to consider making this the foundation of the ongoing evaluation process?

Bob Rhodes. July 2012.

Can life be simply branded as lots of commodities?

Yesterday I was in a Northern city. In terms of what I have to say I could have been a guest of local government in lots of places but yesterday that is where I was. I had been asked to contribute to a session by two wonderful support broker friends – who are also committed members of the National Support Brokerage Network - who had been asked to organise some by a local social care commissioner. The City Council it seemed wanted to hear about Support Brokerage and its relevance to their plans in implementing self directed support and the wider personalisation agenda. They planned to invite both their own key personnel and partners from the providers sector and bannered the session as training, locating the event in the council's training facility.

We had started planning the event and as things progressed enquired as to what fees and expenses this large public body which employs very large numbers was expecting to pay for our skills and knowledge. "There isn't any money for this", they said but we, keen to influence thinking, went ahead. Before the session started and people set their mobile distraction devices to stimulating silent vibration mode (don't ask me where they keep them) some took calls and advised folk that they were at 'training', so could they call back later?

To my mind education and training is, at least in part, concerned with the acquisition of knowledge and skills. We weren't naive – we recognised that the session was implicitly 'contracted' as a shop window for us to show case our services. But equally we are passionate about what we do and in our belief that support brokerage is a simple and self evident set of principles that are accessible to and applicable by everyone – not something to be occupied and professionalised by self-interested workers and organisations.

We set out with experiential exercises and stories to demonstrate the benefits of helping folk get clear about how they want to live despite their difficulties, understanding the essential components of a decent life that can only derive from relationships and the resulting social capital, thinking creatively generating lots of possibilities before finalising any plan, remedying loneliness and isolation, and promoting community association. Finally we repeatedly stressed the importance of a starting stance of seeking to find sustainable ways of helping people achieve their expectations by exploring relationships, associations, and community assets – the counterpoint to the general tendency to see all solutions in paid for services. And we reinforced the message that the principles and key guidelines associated with support brokerage can be understood and implemented, sometimes with enabling support, by just about everyone.

This was not what a lot of our audience were there to glean. The most senior Council officer attending, after introducing the event by majoring upon there being no money for new initiatives (we pointed out repeatedly that there is loads of cash that can be applied very differently and more effectively – a lot was seeming sat unproductive in the room) and describing a number of 'personalisation lite' initiatives in which he was involved, was seen to continuously finger his device and dominate group exercises before needing to leave early. After his own session a colleague observed that he only appeared to fully engage in order to ask about the hourly rate charged by brokers.

An assertive voluntary sector leader, as we broke into groups for "how might we take the principles of support brokerage forward" end session, protested, with support from a colleague, that we had not said anything about principles. When we demonstrated that that was pretty much all we had explored that morning it was quickly apparent that what she really meant was that, in the event that the Council should tender a contract for the provision of Support Brokerage services, we had not provided a template for organisation to bid successfully. I replied, "Hiyo ni nini ni kuhusu" – well, actually I didn't but I might as well have been speaking Swahili because those of us who believe that social services are only valid as supplementary and complementary to what individuals, families, friends and communities do best in reciprocity do speak a different tongue to those who have been groomed throughout their careers in the acid consumer rhetoric of the social market. It's not their fault any more than the integrity of any citizen who doesn't think to question the incongruity of an inherited monarchy within a professed democracy should be impugned. But it is sad.

Many public service workers I met yesterday came along to find out how to specify – that is commodify – and may be one day effectively let a franchise for a company to profit from something we can educate most people to do for themselves or others. Many others came along to prepare themselves to exploit a business opportunity. How perverse!

Here's the chorus!

It's the toughest of commissions
To reverse such powerful trends
Fighting the persuasive grooming
On which commerce still depends

And some new verses for that song:

She's both business-like and power-dressed
A social entrepreneur who's dared
To package family, friends, community
The free love we all once shared

Into products that make profits
Agents of social control
So we all can go on shopping
And forget our heart and soul.

Bob Rhodes

He's a smart suit and an ipad
Knows the price but not the cost
And he's built a big career
On the human rights we've lost

When he's told the hurt he's spawning
Pleads great burdens that he bears
But he's no more credibility
Than the garish ties he wears!

Doing the Right Thing

It's very hard to sustain clear and positive thoughts about social care professionals when you hear such a lack of empathy around a situation where someone is so distressed they put themselves at risk. Time and time again I come across a "professional" who will ignore the distress of a client and focus on ensuring that procedures are followed come what may. Recently, I was working with a young woman (Emily - not her real name) who has numerous significant health issues which were not being resolved and she had ended up confined to her bed in a small bedroom for over 2 years. The lack of any healthcare plan had resulted in Emily requiring high levels of care and had led to social isolation from friends, as his parents increasingly became the main carer and only social contact. I was asked by Emily to visit and offer some advice and guidance with arranging "care" so her Mum and Dad could have a break and because his Mum was about to go into hospital for a major operation which would leave her in the house, without support, for a minimum of four weeks. My initial work was to be helping Emily to make an application to temporarily increase her Personal Budget so a live-in carer could be arranged for the time her Mum was in hospital and for a short period afterwards, whilst she recovered from the operation. After my first visit the presenting facts made me feel uneasy and after discussing the content of the my first meeting with a colleague realised that the Emily was on the autistic spectrum and this was the most significant aspect in respect of her ability to positively engage with health and social care professionals and therefore have any chance of getting better. Eventually this observation was confirmed by the Social worker who, when asked, looked back over the electronic file to find references to Aspergers and "Emily is on the Autistic Spectrum" although nobody seemed to understand that this is why all the professionals were "challenged" by how Emily communicated and the negative impact of stress on Emily's physical and mental health.

Over the next few weeks I (yet again!) got caught in the crossfire between Social and health professionals, who each wanted the other to take financial responsibility. Nobody seemed to understand that Emily needed absolute reassurance that care would be arranged quickly so her Mum could go and have her operation without feeling she has abandoned her daughter and that doing this smoothly would be the best way of limiting the levels of stress for Emily. The reality was, the more Emily got stressed the more she made explicit demands on the Social Worker and her manager who then responded by being more and more defensive about what could and couldn't be agreed. In the end I supported Emily to arrange the live-in care and after a lot of pressure from me the Local Authority eventually agreed the additional Personal Budget five days before Emily's Mum went into hospital. At the same time Emily was having regular email communication with the healthcare professionals regarding the Continuing Health Care assessment which was finally put on hold so the assigned Nurse could grasp the complexity of the situation taking "on board" the Autism label and to make the necessary arrangements directly with Emily to undertake his assessment. However, Emily's Autism related behaviours continued to appear not be taken into account in the by both the social and health professionals. By this time Emily was very stressed and exhausted by the process, resulting in a breakdown in her health which led to an emergency hospital admission five days after her Mum was admitted to hospital. I discovered she had been admitted to hospital three days later when I was due to visit her at home. The immediate response from the managers within Social work was to inform Emily that her care would be immediately withdrawn - no mention of the increased stress which the hospital admission was going to give Emily or even an enquiry about her health! The one thing Emily knew was, with no Mum or Dad around to support her, and the only people she knew and trusted being the care staff which she had employed to support her at home, was to insist they stay supporting her whilst she was in hospital. This created another unnecessary conflict with the social work managers who insisted I collude with their decision and arrange for this care to be withdrawn: I declined. Ironically, the care provider's contract meant they would be paid whether they supported Emily or not! So they stayed. The senior social worker also phoned me to put blame at my door for not telling him about Toby's admission to hospital before I even knew.

Being in hospital created a whole new set of problems as Emily insisted her condition was not being nursed correctly because all the hospital staff were rushing all the medical procedures she needed which resulted in her suffering unnecessary pain and discomfort - so Emily phoned an independent nursing agency and arranged for nurses to come into the hospital to undertake all her procedures. The hospital did not challenge this and after three weeks of these nurses coming into the hospital Emily had run up a bill of over £3,000. The Ward Sister denied that her staff hurried the procedures which led to the increased pain for Emily, but acknowledged it was a very busy ward and they did not have a problem with external agency nurses being employed by one of their patients. I did manage, with the help of Emily's Mum & Dad to convince Emily that having external agency nurses was not affordable and that the Nurses on the ward should be capable of taking their time when administering her medication, although there continues to be issues in this area. The challenge now is around the hospital's desired to discharge Emily without addressing all of her health needs or having a clear negotiated plan for when she is at home. The most recent communication Emily had with the Consultant was that she may need to be sectioned before being discharged to a nursing home: both of which are horrifying prospects for Emily.

The real issues that are placing mental blocks on all the professionals relate to Emily's history of falling out with them after they ignore her views or if they have a meeting about her when she is not involved in some way. Interestingly, Emily has a Personal Budget which is meant to enable the recipient to take more control and be more creative, involving professionals with full consultation and having some sort of consensus on a way forward. Emily is a very intelligent person who, due to her Autism, when stressed, presents in a way which can alienate others and be self destructive. As professionals we all know this, yet in this case, the majority of the professionals appear to act as though Emily is being deliberately obstructive and therefore treat her according to that assessment. I witnessed one conversation between Emily and the Ward Sister in which she wanted to stop the nurses recording that she was refusing fluids, when, as she said to the Ward Sister, she always gives a reason to the Nurse for not being able to drink, which was usually because it was giving her intensive pain. The Ward Sister was reluctant to do this as "my nurses do not have time to write down everything a patient says". This of course leads to more stress for Emily and then the inevitable breakdown in relationships and further deterioration in her health and emotional well-being. It's a vicious circle which could have devastating consequences for Emily. If only, all professionals could just do the right thing which takes into account Emily's very specific, but complex requirements, maybe, just maybe a different and more positive outcome could be achieved which will help her to have the Good Life she really wants!

Colin Campbell January 2013

A Public Health Model of Social Care Regulation?

I recently attended a conference in Denmark convened by friends who, in my opinion, are leading proponents of skilled, reflective, well-observed, and humanely valuing support to people who, for understandable reasons, are usually defined by their distressing and/or threatening behaviours.

One of the star turns at the event was a charming and urbane antipodean who was accorded a slot of 90 minutes to proudly and none too modestly describe his role in what, as it unfolded, seemed to me a thoroughly misconceived extension of a State's annexation of roles and responsibilities that would be better exercised by families who would, if it was widely accepted that they have the primary responsibility for the well-being and safety of their loved-one, make the difference that the machinery of regulation repeatedly appears to miss. In writing this I am in no way deprecating the messenger who was, quite legitimately, crowing about his personal achievements and, I stress, the *potential* for more effective statutory interventions. He functions within a professional, political and bureaucratic hegemony that takes seriously its responsibility for fixing, as 'it' sees it, an incompetent and sometimes wicked world. He is, as I see it, a spoke in a wheel that is constrained by its limited design. It can only travel in a linear way. Like Dyson's vacuum cleaner, when it comes to revisualising social care regulation we need machinery with the fluidity of ball or globe motion.

When the time came for questions I could not resist, as I put it at the time, being "naughty". Our speaker, though I must confess that I could not grasp the connection (other than a probably unjustifiable suspicion that implicit to every apparatchik's socialisation lies a compulsion to extend his or her control and influence), had promulgated a notion that what I had heard as an 'experts and the State know what's best for everyone' construct might merge into a mechanism through which 'public health' is mediated. So I spelt out the following scenario.

Public Health, as I presented it, is significantly concerned with educating, supporting and encouraging citizens to make health enhancing lifestyle choices. I pointed out that, where psychological and behavioural health is concerned, there is a wealth of evidence-based advice on which public health campaigns might be founded. I proposed that consistent public policy would recognise ensuring loving and caring relationships, family, friends, belonging and the social capital that derives from these as a valid priority for everyone.

I started by say that shedloads of research and human empathy inform us that the building blocks of feeling safe and secure are:

- Loving and caring, reciprocal and unconditional relationships and the sense of belonging and wealth of social capital this elicits
- Sufficient economic security to afford some choice
- Opportunities for contributing citizenship
- A place or some might say home which is mine and I can be myself.

Then I proposed that if we had to apply a public health model in accordance with securing the safety and security of people deemed "vulnerable" we would have to set out by acknowledging that services, governments, professionals and institutions don't enjoy a great track record in securing these outcomes. We would have to recognise that families and friendship networks are the most successful deliverers of these outcomes.

Therefore, given that Public Health initiatives are primarily concerned with encouraging citizens to adopt life affirming behaviours, it would be logical and truly professional:

- to launch campaigns that discourage indiscriminate outsourcing of caring responsibilities to "experts" and paid strangers,
- to reinforce the crucial role of families, friends and communities in the lives of "vulnerable" people – as advocates as well as carers and friends – and stressing that "vulnerable" is often a synonym for lonely, neglected and isolated,
- and exposing the limitations as well as the talents to be associated with specialisms and services.

I'm sure that our speaker was as nonplussed as he appeared. To his credit he neither mocked nor expressed sadness over my deviance but it was clear that, within the bounds of his very concrete grasp upon reality, I had commended making soup with stones.

Bob in full flow...

Cormac Russell tells this story which, I'd hazard, is traditional:

A refugee in a hot and dusty country is dependent upon the hospitality of communities he passes through as he seeks his dispersed family, a new place to settle down and some means of earning a living. He arrives this day in a village that has been ravaged by drought. The hospitality for which the people of the area are celebrated has been replaced by closed doors, threatened and threatening looks, and the revival of ancient vendettas. There will be no sustenance to be had here this day.

The traveller collects wood and grasses and builds a fire. From his pack he produces a pot, adds water from the well, and sets the pot upon the fire. In just a few minutes he has a curious audience who gawp in astonishment when he searches around and returns with three large smooth pebbles and drops them carefully into the boiling water. “What are you cooking”, they ask. “Beautiful stone soup”, our traveller replies. “But you can’t make soup with stones”, they exclaim. “Little do you know”, he teases, “but you need not take my word for it. There will be plenty for us all. It would be all the better for a little salt but I have none.”

A woman disappeared and in a jiffy returned with a pinch of salt and the traveller thanked her with a hug. “It’s a shame I’ve had to make this without onions”, he murmured, “but it will still be very nourishing”. Someone else hustled away and in a moment returned with onions that people skinned, sliced and added to the pot. By now there was a lot of to-ing and fro-ing as it seemed that everyone felt the urge to add their small contribution to the pot. Root vegetables, dried pulses, fresh leaves, herbs and spices, potatoes, and even a little dried meat were stirred into the brew and, less than an hour later, the people of the village ate and celebrated together, and agreed that stone soup was indeed as beautiful as the traveller had promised.

It seems to me that the State, by erroneously asserting its competence to keep citizens safe (and especially those made most vulnerable by its incompetence), actively gets in the way of the competent, that is those who are bound by the ties that bind, from asserting and acting forcefully on their primary responsibility to assure the best interests of their loved ones. In my view every healthy and sustainable society is underpinned by the expectation that we all have a part to play as loving advocates and caring contributors who add value to each others' lives. The aping of consumer culture by public services has seriously undermined this ethic as the glue that secures interdependence has been degraded by so many other antisocial solvents.

In my model the State has a raft of vital supplementary, complementary and supportive roles – the first being to ensure that those people made vulnerable by exclusion, lovelessness, and loneliness have these most fundamental issues remedied.

In my unfolding regulatory framework the logistical challenge is to deliver a sustainable, credible and comprehendible system that screams out that supported people and those they look to for natural advocacy constitute the power, the 'parliament' of the system, with the machinery of State as their servant. Families and friends will be clear that they not only enjoy the right but also the responsibility to participate in the monitoring and evaluation of the services used by their loved ones. The State's responsibility will be to organise and support the exercising of these responsibilities and to act as enforcer when asked to by local citizen panels that believe that more than negotiated agreements are required. Officers will undertake investigations, performance improvement activities, and the prosecution/ decommissioning of services in support of caring advocates – with clear accountability to panels of engaged carers. They will also participate in and commission "Catching People Getting It Right" evaluation and enhancement teams of proven and experienced carers and practitioners that will support providers who are committed to improvement.

I have no compunction in highlighting public institutions' astounding competence when it comes to complicating, compromising, bureaucratizing, redefining and eventually scuppering progressive and democratizing initiatives. Institutions accrue power like a Prader Willy compulsive and suffer terribly when constrained to desist. If the fundamental objectives of such a policy change are to be realised, an almost unprecedented emphasis on principled political, strategic, principled, and tenacious leadership will be required and, crucially, a determination to achieve these ends iteratively will be essential. Moves to cross all the t's must be determinedly resisted. Relationships and reciprocity are the language of community, of citizens. Institutions will need to shelve their contractual language if they are to be able to communicate with and truly serve their citizens.

The significant optimism that I attach to the practicality of my proposals derives in part from the housing world. Leasehold Residents Associations in association with principled and ambitious site services agencies are daily demonstrating how communicating and reciprocating residents and tenants can both improve their own lives and those of communities around them. A simple conversation leading to a decision to employ a resident caretaker in place of disconnected external contractors has massively improved the physical environment and the sociability in our West Wales development, and our relationship with our service organisation.

I haven't mentioned what drove me to record these thoughts. Our expert speaker told us that he was travelling on to meet with the Department of Health in the UK. Experience tells us that our institutions are often magnetically attracted to exotic ideas in equal measure to their resistance to many locally evolved proposals. I don't subscribe to the view that this has anything to do with the attractions of exploratory jaunts.

They will not control us – we will be victorious?

I was one amongst the hundreds of millions who watched the 2012 Olympics opening pageant on the telly on Friday night. I shared the pre-ordained and ever more conflated view that Danny Boyle and his creative team had pulled it off as the bread and circuses extravaganza unfolded; but I doubt that my glee at what I experienced as a subversion reflected that which was so enthralling the gushing pundits?

It should be no surprise, even if he will likely never publically acknowledge it, that a Director with the wit and insight to make *Train Spotting* and *Slumdog Millionaire* would be unable to resist the opportunity to make a statement and to take a pop at a society that he has so many times exposed as shallow, self-seeking, self-destructive – and manipulated.

So what did Danny tell us, show us, expose? He started with a pastoral idyll of chocolate box villages, cricket, Maypoles and rusticism; a fanciful England that would be sooted and smithed in the fiery filth of industrialisation – an era of achievement, innovation, wealth creation, urbanisation and unprecedented exploitation.

He then gave us tableaux of how, in dire adversity, it is in the spirit of human kind to combine, associate, organise, campaign, subvert; that is revolt. The greatest achievements of the British people were set out as the struggles of labour movement leaders, trades unionists, suffragettes, mutualists and co-operators were portrayed and brought to fruition in a celebration of their greatest legacy, the National Health Service – now no longer run in accordance with its founding culture, local identities and values.

From there on Boyle's piece was – whether intended or not (I sense that it was) - a demonstration of how so many of subsequent generations have frittered away the hard won freedoms, rights, responsibilities and camaraderie secured by their forebears being, in the process, cast back as units of production, consumption punters, the disposable ephemera that exists vicariously and disconnectedly and rarely makes an associational difference. He represented our recent history as a place of omnipresent popular 'culture', characterised by the musical and visual diversions which give us all belonging. A belonging forged in our youths at a time when we were, perhaps, most distant from and deaf to other generations. The technology may evolve and, perhaps, become all the more compelling – suffice it to say that the abiding image Danny left with me was of generations subject to the often mindless outpourings of ever-present and demanding popular culture; defined by fashion, fad, brand allegiance... ephemeral, over-dependent, schooled to be dependent, individualised, commercialised, groomed and, if such perspectives are aired, perplexed.

And who wouldn't be perplexed by a society where in order to raise cash for good causes – where you have no affiliation to the good causes helped nor even what defines a good cause – it is legitimate to dispense money to a hundred new millionaires on one night having, very largely, taken that hundred million pounds from working families who often cannot really afford to enter the raffle? Or where televised celebrity-fests constitute the main channel for charitable giving – where givers outsource the responsibility for where and how their giving is applied to anonymous others and build neither relationship with nor knowledge of anyone or anything.

But, to return to the 'installation', we were simply presented with a story that recorded the triumph of the common man only to see that progress towards collaboration, cooperation, interdependence, reciprocity, mutuality and participative democracy eroded as the fruits of the struggle, at least initially, opened the door to individualism, self-seeking, materialism, and Epicureanism and to those who would exploit such human frailties and seek to ensure that socialism will be erased from human memory.

And so I mused that Danny left the best jokes to the end. It wasn't the total irrelevance of an insipid McCartney rendering of one of The Beatles' most meaningless anthems that really got me giggling. I was already in bits by then having been floored by the lunacy of The Killers' assertion that,

"They will not control us
We will be victorious",
because, in my head, a voice was singing,
"We are just consumers
Fightbacks are all rumours".

Some time ago I went to Sacramento
And met the vets who beg on downtown streets
Sans limbs dignity their gaze broken low
Ignored by evangelic capital's elites
And talked the talk with those who would bring change
To right the wrongs free poor folk from dread fear
Who organise campaign but no longer think it strange
That there's no talk of socialism here

Some time ago I thought in Sacramento
Amongst those who would build community
Based on a bold unalienable credo
We all have gifts that we can share for free
And as I thought with them in Sacramento
Fine people strong in spirit ever kind
I chewed on how our place can make a 'no go'
Of forbidden fruits we must not call the mind

We're capitalists down here in Sacramento
There is no other Christian way to be
Co-operators levellers non-conformists showed us how to row
To a deep contrary dock called liberty
Where we've freedom of contract given reason to fear
Those we elect who assert most forcefully
That the law succours wealth costs the people rights dear
Rewards those who exploit and lie remorselessly

It's un-American in Sacramento
To insist that life's more than transactions
It's all about dough so go with the flow

God knows how God copes with the factions
Who insist that freedom's dynamic
Is essentially just economic
Whose vision is not panoramic
Whose principles are palindromic

A right scary place is Sacramento
Reflecting a cultural cancer
So it's best if you can be content to
Quote dogma seek no other answer
If you do then accept you aren't free
To propagate any conclusion
That suggests there's more to liberty
Or postulates redistribution

Birthright to think persuade and associate
Great triumph of folk in these islands
Not a deal we should renegotiate
A treasure beyond diamonds
But they've lost it in the States
Where belief is bought and sold
Annexing nationalism and faith
The brand exploiters uncontrolled

History's lessons could not be more clear
Constant struggle of the common man
the moment we suspend the fight
the ruling elites strike back
so we can't take our foot off the pedal
be alert
associate organise and agitate

On the Care Market – A Parody (Bob Rhodes)

I'll buy you some nice home care my dear
Just to see that you're alright
Fit you out with help alarms no fear
To see you through the night
We haven't got a lot of money
Three short calls should be alright

Your days seem endless
Let's try and find a charity
You're feeling friendless
So have a nice strong cup of tea

I wish I had the time I'd love to chat
About your life and deeds
But I've a questionnaire I know off pat
Assessing all your needs
And if you want some of our money
You'd best put on your widow's weeds

It's best that you should know before we start
There's no points for your gifts
Tell me from the heart before we part
Your frailties, faults and rifts
I've got to justify the money
That's the way the process shifts

No need to feel cowed
You can always self-direct
I'll tell you what's allowed
It won't be what you should expect

And I can't help you if you get too funny
Or get your pushy family round
In the end it's 'public money'
Doesn't pay to break new ground

If you had a choice I'd make a guess
You'd choose to stay round here
Doing church and club with Cec and Bess
Give your grandkids a steer
But we've committed all the money
Commissioning big care homes dear

Can't buy you love dear
A transaction beyond me
Can buy you care dear
Not too clear what that might be
You should invest dear
Start to read the old FT
Life's just a bitch dear
Have a nice strong cup of tea
And I shouldn't count on me!
Have a nice strong cup of tea
And I shouldn't count on me...

Businesses and Bosses who help families and community to get tax exemptions – A Daft Idea?

I often have these contrapuntal moments. Do you? Occasionally the same discomfort irritates my semi-consciousness, a hungry midge around the top of moist socks in the syrup of a sultry evening. I carry on with life but as soon as I allow myself to sink back relaxed the itch intensifies and demands attention - hot, swollen, sometimes suppurating always spiky, somehow irresolvable.

The itch might usually be christened Why? – with the question mark imperative like those titles snorted onto rock icons' vulnerable infants, whose younger siblings are starred to be named How? and Oh Shit! The questions wriggling to burst out so countervalent, so contrary and surreal, but in the same instant so incisive. Is it the same for you?

Such is this rash of orgasmic itches, so demanding of exploring touches, impossible to satisfy, resolve. I muse about the possibility that we all see the contradictions, illogic, inequity, inhumanity and sometimes abject lunacy in the non-negotiables that circumscribe our existence.

Anyway, let's get down to it. Here's the nub of my thoughts and ramblings, my itch:

It seems that people have no longer any time to care for each other. If they are, it is said, "fortunate" both partners in a relationship work long hours in order to be successful participants in consumer society. The consequence is that we have outsourced many of the activities associated with caring. As what used to be relational, a matter of duty and love, has become occupational and professional, the definition of care has insidiously changed. For instance, child care is now specified as an educational activity, subject to a raft of institutionally imposed targets, for which most parents are unqualified. Not only have the unqualified been excluded from the activity as a result of its professionally mediated re-specification. Other loving and competent parents are also deemed unsuited by reason of the safeguarder's credo that, "You can't trust anyone – don't only lock up your daughters, confine your children to the safety of your kraal."

Nor have we sufficient time for our elders and the further we've separated from them, for many, the more unwholesome they (I mean we – as I'm sort of retired) seem. And we've even less time for our neighbours, our friends, cousins, aunts and the rest who wouldn't wish to burden us, would feel it wrong to ask and just, when it's their turn, suffer in silence.

It seems that we've plenty of time for our holidays, Nintendo's, game stations, and gyms. And we make enough time for times with our mates and some for more unfaithful dates. Plus, there's just enough time to go shopping, consuming online and in-store, and just enough time for TV or a good DVD if it is poor. The justification for our recreation is the stress work exerts...on our lives - mind, body and limbs.
One might be forgiven for thinking that grown human beings don't really want to care for each other, see this as something of a low status activity, a bit below them and at the same time demanding of empathy and interpersonal skills at a level way out of their league?

But, on the other hand, just a couple of generations ago – while it may be right to assert that gender roles were unnecessarily functionally defined – most of us worked harder in more punishing conditions and then went home to poorer nutrition - to dig in the garden or allotment so that we could eat better; in the countryside to bury the night soil from the Elsan; to our roles in religious, mutual and neighbourhood organisations; and to our day-to-day roles in caring for those in our extended families and communities. Surely we cannot have exchanged our humanity for the sado-masochistic chains of illusory consumption irrevocably?

So, one of my itches stings me to suggest that, given a fighting chance, most of us retain the germ of a determination to love and stay loyal to those who have loved and struggled for us? If this is so the challenge is to stir that germ to germinate and grow sturdy.

Similarly my work in social care screams at me that if and when the time comes for any of us to cope with the bumpy roads of life we are exponentially richer if we have family, friends and community to accompany us on the journey.

To my mind we are presently flailing around in a vicious vortex. We work to earn to spend to feed growth in order to generate profit to be invested to create jobs so that people can earn to spend and so ad infinitum. Concurrently owners and investors have first call on profits that may be all the greater if their businesses are more efficient which often means less jobs, more demanding or mind-numbingly tedious work, less wages pro rata of time worked and the likelihood that jobs will be located where costs are least. Lots of people work harder and harder in mindless pursuit of redundancy.

Meanwhile Governments are taxing businesses in order to fund their programmes which, to a significant extent, are concerned how we care for each other – the very activities that State has taken on because we say we're too busy competing in the consumer dog eat rat race to sort out ourselves.

We need to break the vicious vortex that links commercial viability for businesses with more and more demands upon the undivided and exclusive time and attention of their employees. (Concurrently, and I imagine a more challenging commission, we need to break the cultural link between time spent not working for wages and having recreation)

Presently there is precious little connection between most employers and the families of those they employ. In only rare cases do employers adopt a very engaged corporate social responsibility stance in regard of those communities from which their employees derive. There are few if any of the like of Robert Adams, Rowntree, Cadbury, Lever or even George Dowty in the contemporary business world and farmers, estate owners, mine owners and their equivalents in the public services sphere now restrict their attention to market imperatives, the disciplines of the single balance sheet. The triple bottom line – profitability, social responsibility, and ecological rigour – is rarely the defining issue in the boardroom.

But we need employers who do care about their employees' wellbeing and understand that this is rooted in the stability of their family lives and the vigour of their communities.

So here's the BIG IDEA.

Let's significantly reduce the burden of taxation and underwrite the employers' contributions to infrastructural employment costs for any employer who is prepared to, Semler-like, support their workers so that they may be caring and contributing family members and contributors to resourceful and reciprocal communities in transparent and democratic partnerships with workers councils elected to develop and oversee locally relevant arrangements.

The freed up monies may be applied very creatively – that means without the creeping red tape that usually accompanies liberalising initiatives in the UK – but will generally be applied initially to support the responsive "over-staffing" necessary to facilitate and accommodate more reciprocal and communitarian employment practices.

Key indicators of the efficacy of the policy will include:

- Reduced demands upon public services – specifically those associated with child care, social care, juvenile crime and health
- Evidence of increased association and reciprocity in the communities affected

- Stronger – more resourceful, resilient and self-reliant - citizens, families and local communities.

ABOUT RICARDO SEMLER

Ricardo Semler, author and business manager, is celebrated as a role model of a Chief Executive who breaks all the traditional rules and succeeds, massively.

Semler eliminated what he called 'corporate oppression" from his company, Semco: time clocks, dress codes, security procedures, privileged office spaces and perks, they all went. There were to be no receptionists or secretaries.

He set up 'factory committees' to run the plants, in an attempt to get more worker involvement and Semler guaranteed that no-one could be fired while serving on the committees or for at least a year afterwards.

Ricardo then introduced profit-sharing schemes for all the workers. The thought that they could directly influence their own pay encouraged the committees to look for savings and to question any procedures or layers of management that didn't seem to add value.

Managers were hired and fired by their own employees. More than that, the units were now inventing new businesses for themselves. And so Semco grew, entirely due to the initiatives of its workers.

The workers have unrestricted access to all corporate records and are taught how to read financial reports; they set their own wages and their own production quotas.

When the number of people in a Semco unit hits the 100 to 200 mark it is split in two, like it or not.

Semler lists six principles that guide his always experimental company:

1. don't increase business size unnecessarily
2. never stop being a start-up
3. don't be a nanny to your workers
4. let talent find its place

5. make decisions quickly and openly
6. partner promiscuously, you can't do it all yourself.

Limerick – Let's vote Rikki Semler for President

Let's vote Rikki Semler for President
Notorious Brazilian resident
A true maverick
Who gets on the wick
Of those bosses employees resent

Let's vote Rikki Semler to lead
Such a visionary it's agreed
Who makes autonomy
Weather vane of the free
A priority over greed

Let's vote Rikki Semler to show
Our fey posers the right way to go
Abandon the in-crowd
PPE's to be disallowed
Try trusting the people to know

Rikki knows our elite isn't ruling
It's the unseen controllers we're duelling
Who make markets groom cultures
Then clean up like vultures
Who do they think they are fooling?

Let's vote Rikki Semler and boast
Of our talents from mountain to coast
No longer repressed
Our passions expressed
The book cooking crooks will be toast

Let's vote Rikki Semler and take
The chance to love care and make
Our lives more than shopping
Endless toil disco bopping
And from our long nightmare awake

A Lesson from the Lottery

Last night, after dinner and a stroll around the bay with the dogs, I found myself curled up with a cup of tea half attending to the Saturday Lottery TV programme. A mother and daughter, whose aspirations in life were stated as spending a lot of money on a wedding plus shed loads of designer shoes and handbags, competed for and won one hundred thousand pounds on the basis of their knowledge of the dates of birth of celebrities' children, the dates of demise of fictional soap characters, and their ignorance of the bones in their bodies and world geography. It made me think. It was a source of profound anger and sadness. I found myself mouthing clichés at my wife – "Is this what we've come to?"

Over recent weeks the National Lottery has devoted a lot of time to congratulating itself on its sponsorship of Olympic athletes. In this programme, with that event passed, it moved on to Paralympians and I got to thinking about how this got to be a priority and how decisions about how these allegedly charitable funds are administered. It struck me that, assuming you take the easily justified view that every form of state (every manifestation of democracy included) exists to protect the privileges of the powerful and to effect this coercion as invisibly and 'benignly' as possible, the National Lottery is a tailor-made tool.

Commoditisation at work

The powerful whose privileges our state exists to promote and protect are those who benefit from a commercial, capitalist economy and society. When capitalism surveys any transaction it applies, as it perceives it, a preordained and irrefutable logic that converts needs and wants into commodities than can be taken to the market. The Lottery is simply a nifty mechanism for commoditising charity, as are telethons such as Comic Relief and Children in Need (doesn't it strike you as odd that, despite the publicity around the 'problem', we haven't seen the emphasis changed to 'Demented (or Clinically Obese) and in Need'?), in the fundamental sense that they enable the outsourcing and depersonalisation of charity, and then alienate and romanticize altruism. And all in the true spirit of capitalism! You pay your money, take your incredibly long odds chance of unconscionable levels of winnings, rationalise your expenditure as a charitable gift (despite less than 20% getting to 'good causes'), may be don't even realise that you are participating in what is essentially another form of regressive taxation as government has undue influence on how funds are disbursed, and, most importantly, outsource your altruism and institutionalise what could be your personal responsibility – perhaps ending up more consumer and less human?

Meanwhile the Lottery franchisees take their profits and their shareholders their dividends. And you don't see too many affluent folk queuing to register their numbers?

Outsourcing our lives, after successfully taking control!

John McKnight and others have demonstrated how we have succumbed to and been complicit in the outsourcing of 'care' or, in its wider sense, social welfare.

"Professionalisation is the market replacement for a community that has lost or outsourced its capacity to care. The loss of community competence is the price we pay for the growth of the service economy"
John McKnight and Peter Block – The Abundant Community (p36)

Martin Buber and Colin Ward add a European perspective to this analysis in explaining how, after the Second World War, many states, and notably Britain, overtly rebranded their central role as the provision of social welfare in the face of the grassroots communitarian and mutualist challenges to the power and authority of the state that had begun in the late 19th century, gained impetus given the treasonable mistreatment of the "heroes" of World War 1, and been honed by the industrial and economic calamities that culminated in the great depression, hungry 30's and yet another war to end all wars.

"Buber provided a striking polarization of the two principles of human behaviour involved: the political and the social. He saw the characteristics of the political principle to be power, authority, hierarchy, and dominion, while the social principle was visible to him in all spontaneous human associations built around a common need or a common interest"
Colin Ward

(He concluded that), *"All forms of government have this in common: each possesses more power than is required by the given conditions; in fact, this excess for making dispositions is actually what we understand by political power. The measure of this excess...represents the exact difference between administration and government."*
Martin Buber

During these years people appreciated the irrationality of depending upon governments that primarily represent the interests of the powerful and so associated and organised really important stuff for themselves. Social insurance, social housing, health insurance, and a plethora of local charities, mutual aid societies, allotments associations, reading rooms, friendly societies, youth organisations and, of course, effective, grassroots trades unions were all a consequence of the genius and resourcefulness of ordinary people unfettered and in need. Bevan described this blossoming of social spontaneity as more the consequence of "Methodism than Marxism". Every initiative starts when "two or three gather together", "When people care enough to Act". The most telling way of enchaining a population resides in removing any need to associate and act. It could be that such a strategy would be strengthened by keeping folk preoccupied by trivia, ephemera, fashion and football?

I would stress that it would be a mistake to view the institutionalisation and statutory leadership of social welfare by the Atlee and subsequent governments as malign or conspiratorial. However we want to describe the environment against which various affiliations of political practitioners struggle to serve, and no matter how organised some elements of powerful interests are, the concepts of "powerful elites", "ruling elites", and capitalists or capitalism should not be personalised. It is more helpful as I see it to envisage it as a powerful force that is in constant interaction with other environmental forces. However, since time immemorial, powerful elites have controlled states. The biggest threat to powerful elites lies in the populace deciding that the state is contrary to their wellbeing and either marginalising it or doing away with it altogether. Post 1945 the force that emanates from power simply accepted that, for the time being, coercion was likely to be a counterproductive strategy. Turning self help initiatives into statutory services and rights, telling folk, "you don't need to worry anymore, leave it to us, we'll look after you and lift responsibilities from your shoulders", was a great compromise to be 'managed' until an unintended consequence, consumerism and generalised dependency, offered both irresistible temptations and more unintended consequences of the challenging variety that could portend a return to more coercive inevitabilities?

By the time Harold McMillan was boasting that the British had "never had it so good" the political imperative for a welfare state had become a 'burden' that UK governments of all persuasions have been intent upon dismantling from the 1950's but with gusto since the Thatcher regime of the 1980's despite

the paradox that apparent adherence to its principles have remained the lingua franca of detached representative politics.
In his "Leaderless Revolution" Carne Ross demonstrates how we have also succumbed to outsourcing or contracting out our personal political power. Commenting on how politics seems ever more to be reduced to one-sided, disconnected, single issue lobbying and campaigning professionally- led not for profit businesses he observes that, *"Whereas active participation in community organisations correlates with political participation, there are no such "positive externalities" of paying membership dues to a non-profit. In essence we are contracting out politics to be done by others".*

And he concludes that this cannot and will not continue. *"Today we are too accustomed to distrusting one another, to perceiving the "other" at home or abroad as hostile or malign. We are too accustomed to letting government take care of matters...But if it's true the government is less and less able to manage our collective affairs, it seems that we have little choice but to take that burden on our own shoulders. We must learn anew to produce the effects we desire, to take responsibility for ourselves, and for others, and to cooperate and negotiate with each other, instead of leaving that arbitration to an evidently imperfect mechanism."*

We might quickly disregard these perspectives if they came from outside the establishment, but they don't! Mr Ross represented the UK, on key issues such as climate change, terrorism, and the wars in Afghanistan and Iraq (where he led for the UK) at the United Nations. He "*realised that perhaps the worst deficit of government was this: in claiming to arbitrate the world's problems, unintentionally it encourages our own inaction and detachment".*

And, if we leave it to Carne's *"current cohort of lousy politicians"* we actively collude with their implicit addiction to the market society that is the playground of the powerful (whoever or whatever they may be).

The Problem with Social Enterprise

In 2003, in my speech when I received a Social Entrepreneur of the Year award, I confessed surprise at my recognition given that, as far as I could see, I wasn't a Social Entrepreneur but rather someone who provided a different conduit for the application of public monies. I thought that, in general, people benefitted significantly from the personal and relationship focused way in which we went about our work and that we were probably due some sort of good practice award but, for me, social enterprise meant garnering social benefits from commercial activities – for instance, creating businesses that provide rewarding and properly remunerated employment for disabled or long-term unemployed folk.

It has only gradually dawned on me - as I've watched so many statutory functions rebranded as social enterprises, so many 'insiders' peddle and pitch allegedly self-financing ideas inside Downing Street and Cardiff Dock, Think Tanks cream off others' initiatives and get reborn as expert consultancies, and the barely camouflaged drive to force NFP mergers and purge the social welfare market place of anything other than big, balance sheet obsessed players – that I was engaged in social enterprise in 2003 as I was administering large amounts of public money with barely any public accountability. Now, in fact we were, though this was never in the service specification with the oomph that we applied, working hard to individualise the funds we received on behalf of folk and involving them and their loved ones more and more in applying their allocations in pursuit of their goals and often arbitrarily varying the contract. However, those service specifications did not recognise the service user as the contractor – another paradox?

And as this dawned on me I reflected on my times as a senior manager and budget holder in statutory bodies and concluded that I was not really subject to any real accountability for how I apportioned public funds in those roles either. The system concentrated on control rather than quality and getting 'it' right rather than doing the right thing. The struggle, whichever side of the fence one found oneself, was the get away with doing the right thing.

Martin Buber – 'Society and the State' – in M Buber – Pointing the Way RKP 1957
Colin Ward – 'Social Policy – An Anarchist Response – LSE 1996

A strategy for self direction... An episode in the life of a Support Broker working with folk who have spent most of their lives in the care system and a Care Provider that cares

Consider your situation. Your parents are dead. Since your mother's funeral six years ago you've only seen your sister twice. There's a card and gift each Christmas and your birthday has been remembered once since then. She's invited to care reviews but doesn't come. Your key worker, Jo, thinks she may have moved but cannot find any reference in your file. Jo is pregnant and taking maternity leave shortly. You'll soon have someone new to take a special interest in you.

You started to go to the hospital when you were little – to give your mum a break. Then they opened a special school at the hospital and you were sent there as you were now deemed educable. You were often angry, lonely and frightened so it was decided that you had better live at the hospital. You didn't get to go home much after that. When you did you made it clear that you didn't want to go back so it was decided that it might best if you didn't go home at all.

This year is your Golden Jubilee. You've been in the care system since 1962 and, starting with Albert Kushlick's heroic experiments in Wessex in the late 60's, things have moved on for you. You no longer have to survive the stresses and anxieties of life on a ward of 50 equally frightened and consequently often unpredictable people, nor the regimens of kind or unfeelingness of unkind and equally institutionalised staff. It was there that you learned to be alone, invisible, unnoticed – best left to your own devices. Now you share your life with 3 other survivors in a nice house with an unkempt garden, a jumble of staff cars overflowing the drive and an ever-changing staff team of around a dozen people. You have found that you can get by here too by being invisible. They have decided that that is how you prefer to live. They don't know how lonely and frightened you are – nor how unfulfilled and bored. From time to time someone comes along and there's a chemistry. You begin to loosen up, to trust, but you know that it won't be long before they move on, they're gone.

It is so obvious. The challenge for social care is not just about where people live; it is concerned with how people live. If we truly want to support people with intellectual disabilities to pursue good lives we have to find out how people want to live and then act upon what they tell us instead of redefining what we are hearing into the menu of things that services already do.

Alongside this we have to be honest about the limitations of services. It's cheesy but Lennon and McCartney were right to point out that love can't be bought and, like it or not, loving and caring reciprocal relationships that give rise to social capital and a sense of belonging are the meat and drink of emotional and practical well-being. Services cannot begin to meet this fundament human need but can partner with those who can and, crucially, be attentive to the unintended consequences of what they do. We can as a beginning set out to make what we do, as Al Etmanski so succinctly put it in *A Good Life*, ensure that our services are "supplementary and complementary". It is when we set out to be the comprehensive solution – the silver bullet of lazy commissioning – that real life is excluded; sadly this is often the current default position.

If we are serious about personalisation, self direction, inclusion and everything that adds up to deinstitutionalising and normalising the lives of disabled people (and everyone else entitled to support in our communities) we have to change our way of working so that we:

- Ask different questions, good life questions, what really matters to you questions
- Do something about ensuring that people have loving and caring reciprocal relationships and the natural advocacy that follows

- Understand that individuals are social beings. People live in the context of interdependency
- Throw away service menus and learn to think and act creatively – using all the resources not just money – in honestly responding to what folk tell us
- Make our services catalysts for community rather than the inert and isolated silos they so frequently are
- Keep the cash in our back pockets to spend on the things that can't be done better in other ways
- As service providers, target earning less per capita year on year as we assist people to be less dependent upon us
- Organise for the long haul – life is a journey, not a succession of bureaucratically convenient episodes.

A telling consequence of adopting and developing this support brokerage informed strategy is that, over time, individual service costs will reduce (by more than a quarter in the small scale evaluations to date), families and communities will be strengthened and the slide towards public services dependency reversed, and, most importantly, lots and lots of excluded people will be restored to contributing citizenship.

Published in Community Living Volume 2 2012

On Leadership

People who are dependent on procedures routines checklists and plans
Seem not to be sentient to the illogic and implicit unpredictability of life
The countervalencies and inconsistencies that litter our conflicted existence
The essential paradox that insists that anything imposed will be subverted
Nor bright enough to stop tightening the screw when the head has disintegrated

Of course it is both unfair and inappropriate to impugn their competence and ethics
As they are organisms who strive to survive and thrive in a cultural ecosystem
A political/institutional hegemony that has successfully adopted a defensive posture
That ranks being procedurally right over getting it right or doing the right thing
And as a consequence folk are constrained from getting appropriately down and dirty

I mused that “Alice in Wonderland” is the perfect allegory for this parallel surreality
A truly amoral conjunction of the bizarre the symbolic the arbitrary and hierarchy
Where purpose is obscure if present at all personal influence the object of existence
And summary extinction a terrifying consequence of misinterpreting arcane customs
In an institution thus immured from the possibility of internal criticism or innovation

And so we might adduce that far too much institutional life is predicated by fear
The loathing and divisiveness that inherently attends upon competition for survival
Status privilege and rewards associated with both pristine and faecal nostrils
By compliance subservience to the litanies and creeds of hierarchical competence
Purpose-free institutions of brown nosed clubbable super-complier survivors?

We are at a point in human history where strong opinions are timely
Frank open-ended humble pundit-free conversations amongst citizens urgent
Squandering our gifts googling and boogying while the earth around us burns
Ignoring tomorrow for short term advantage deferring to the powerful self-interested
We need real leadership because we know it's daft to depend on leaders!

Those paradoxical souls who serve and befriend but are of necessity 1% bastard
Sensing that the progress of humanity is a trial and error journey compromised by the paradox
Of me and us, we and them, my wealth and status, my power and our survival, interdependence
Persuade us to put aside selfish things find joy and warmth in surmounting disasters and
Instead of some bestial foe accept that we are the goose-stepping cohorts in denial

It is said that effecting normative cultural revolution is like turning an oil tanker
It's not, ships have no mind of their own and are turned on an hourly basis and are not programmed
To persist in pursuit of their own disinterest by, shall we fantasize, the salvage companies
While our consumption blinded culture lives beyond sustainability suicidally adolescently compulsively
Delusionally dishonestly soullessly selfishly ignorantly and above all naively and innocently

It's the Toughest of Commissions – A song with many tunes (Calon Lan works best) (or Reflections on Platform 3, Newport, South Wales)

There's a hoarding at the station
That in 12 by 8 proclaims
The joy of urban living
Is that little life remains

Chorus (between each verse and to end)
It's the toughest of commissions
To reverse such powerful trends
Fighting the persuasive grooming
On which commerce still depends

Work Shop Play is its prescription
For contentment in this day
We're habitual consumers
For as long as we can pay

Just forget about tomorrow
Gorge the birthrights of our kids
Loutish ravage feast can't borrow
Planet knackered on the skids

It is a clear reflection
Mirrors that we have lost touch
With the essences of living
Now we don't amount to much

If teachers raise our children
To plans laid down by number ten
And we warehouse our dear grannies
Safeguarded they say by them

If we mustn't trust our neighbours
As professionals know best
We're all wage slaves and we know it
At the money men's behest

The real joy in urban living
Comes when citizens relate
Organise around what matters
Redirect the winds of fate

Rediscover in their trials
Civilisation will renew
When the efforts of the people
Reward all not just a few

When we've love for those who've raised us
Time to be the hands of care
Made a village for our children
Parishes that all can share

So don't succumb to entertainment
Punditry celebrity
Active in association's
Much more satisfactory

Ready for the revolution
That will come unstoppably
When the dispossessed redundant
Exceed those who think they're free

When we're back in nature's kilter
Back in touch with you and me
We will sustain one another
Work Shop Play's dark history

It's the toughest of commissions
To reverse such powerful trends
Fighting the persuasive grooming
On which commerce still depends

Simple Lessons from the U3A

I love to play table tennis and from childhood until my mid-50's - when I mistakenly 'retired' because I no longer commanded the fitness and reflexes of the youngsters nor the gritty consistency of the oldsters to whom I too regularly lost - I played competitively in local leagues wherever we lived, as often as not establishing clubs in our community in the process. Around the same time I had ceased regular commitments as a rugby coach, cut somewhat obsessive gym sessions following joint problems, and persuaded myself that golf and dog walking were now more age-appropriate alternatives.

This year, 7 or 8 years too late, with opportunities for enjoyable golf much abbreviated by our missed carbon reduction climate and the romance of endless forest dog walks dulled by quagmires and soggy fur, I resolved to remedy my error. My wife had recently retired, exploited her release to intensify participation in her passion for dance, and had acquired new interests in badminton and exercise classes. Not only was this physical lifestyle a boon to her physical and emotional wellbeing; as importantly it constituted a brimming well of friendships, acquaintances, social capital and belonging in a community in which she had been a peripheral actor, a weekender. So I contacted my local rugby club, was immediately welcomed and following a couple of conversations allocated responsibility for a junior squad for the coming season. Table-tennis, however, posed bigger challenges. Googling away I eventually had to concede that table-tennis and the Forest of Dean are not synonymous. The nearest possibility seemed to be Ross on Wye where I found and joined a really welcoming club where I play most Tuesdays – my consulting and training lifestyle inevitably means that can't be every Tuesday – and through which I enjoy match play in the Malvern League.

The other possibility arising from my internet search were 3 morning sessions every week organised by the University of the Third Age

(U3A) in Chepstow. I should know better but I had pretty much discounted the relevance of this to my situation. I stereotyped the opportunity as 'recreational' when I wanted to compete and, worse, the mental image I generated was of grey hearty frailty. Still, I made Chepstow U3A a 'favourite' and as soon as I realised that I needed more than my Ross connection to ensure the opportunity of playing at least once a week, resolved to go along and give it a go.

And what a damascene experience that proved! The group has excellent facilities at Chepstow Rugby Club with 4 fast tables and the most deft and facilitating organisation imaginable. During my first two hour session I doubt that I sat down for more than 5 minutes. Within 20 minutes the almost unseen 'coordinators' had assessed my competence, organised a succession of doubles matches with players of similar abilities, and set me to work to coach 'improvers'. I loved it! So I paid £12 so that I can participate in any or all of the 3 sessions every week throughout the year for a £1 sessional fee. "Just one other thing you must do", my greeter said, "that is to join U3A before you come again". I had previously downloaded the application form and agreed to deal with membership expeditiously.

And here we come to the nub of my story. When I got home and read the application form I immediately understood why the morning had been such a joyful experience. The form asked for the usual name, address and contact information; it asked me to identify any of the group's current activities in which I might be interested; and just one other question, what particular interests or expertise had I that I might be willing to share with others, contribute?

Given the deficit laden world of public services that I usually inhabit I was struck by its absence of interest in my age, my dietary proclivities, mobility and access requirements, communication difficulties, ethnicity, marital status, sexual orientation, or economic status. It simply sought to elicit what I might be able to add to the communal pot and implicitly gave me license to make offers. It also signalled that the association would welcome and support such gifts. There was no small print about qualifications, CRB's, references, experience or governance. The Chepstow U3A is semi-autonomous and, while members are elected to voluntary officer roles, organises itself through monthly 'council' meetings at which all members are welcome. It seems to function with a minimum of bureaucracy, a maximum of devolved autonomy to the organisers of its member-led interest groups, and a passionate attachment to the principle that older people are a treasure chest of knowledge, skills, experience, resourcefulness, tenacity and know how. During my first two hours at Chepstow I not only revelled in a sporting feast but observed multiple exchanges of social capital, formations of functional problem solving associations, and the reinforcement of friendship, belonging. In short, U3A seems to be the epitome of an asset based community development association and a thriving example. Maybe public sector leaders should seek their help?

U3A – a parody

Introduction and Chorus

You can show us the way U3A
You can show us the way U3A
You can show us the tricks local leaders can choose
To get happiness in the news!

Old man both your feet on the ground
I say old man with good sense that's renowned
Can you strip the red tape from our everyday ploys
And diminish the background noise?

Old girl with your sense of tough love
I say old girl can you look from above
Make relational sense of our inhuman rules
Give us people-scaled simple tools?

Old folk with perspective to spare
I say old folk who still know how to care
Will you share what you've learned about what matters most
And shout it from coast to coast?

Sitting with George

A life of cider
Slaking hard earned thirst in the fields
The source of recreation loosened tongues
Anaesthesia in the inn of a night
Was as for so many of his generation
To lead to a yellowing then blackening thrashing
An incoherent and undignified departure
Ill-fitted to our shy near silent neighbour

A man of few words
A life defined by manly tasks and obligations
Nurtured by a gentle yet tough and uncomplaining
Helpmate with no great expectations
Other than he would be kind predictable
Put food on the table coal in the grate
Take pride in their sons and grieve as she did
For the tail gunner who never filled the grave she tended

Amongst the first in our near peasant place
To lash out on the television organise their furniture
Cinema-style their front room – she adored children –
Weekdays our first youth club crammed in we were
For children's hour the Cisco Kid, Lone Ranger until
Ten to six when George pedalled past the window
And we would quietly leave before his clips were off
His well oiled bike safe stabled in the shed

A decade or more on and George who I saw spoke to
Every day but never knew is up those stairs I think
I've never climbed yelling rambling sweating dying

And I remember well the day that his pedalling feet had
Passed the window and I called out that "George was home"
Only to be sharply corrected that he was to be called
By Mr and his surname the respect that he deserved
From children even me and the only time in both our lives
That I recalled her voice raised in anger a marker set
While now a callow gauche and blushing youth I was to her a man
So kind to share the death watch with her George support his stoic widow

They all came and whether or not he knew recounted
All the tales epic and mundane sad silly and salacious
Of his life with us especially with them at plough in driving rain

Of long dry dusty harvest days and nights and skittles
Darts the Somme's dark mud stained with the blood
Of Billy, Joe and brother Harry whose allotment
Even as a lad the favourite with the girls was always
A picture double dug no bindweed there or cooch

And all were expected even those intolerable in life
Performed their valued roles in the rites of passing
Notorious drunks beaters of wives as one with the upright
Hellfire lay-preachers the steady strong and silent
Raconteurs and listeners after their day's labour
Neck's scrubbed boots gleaming donned their part
Apprenticed the coming generation bore up the frail
And gave belonging joy deep respect to be in turn reciprocated

I was there when the end came
More silently calmly than seemed possible
Grandson to an undertaker expected so it seemed
To have the knack of soothing others feelings fears
Denying nightmare terrors of my own
It seems I carried this off joined the cider set
And still remember the clanking of the trolley
Passing beneath my window when in the face of prior tradition
They took old George away

Mine was not to be the rhythm of October cider pressings
Our brood never passed the horn communally sorting spuds
Took eggs logs or fresh-pressed brawn to wiry
Wellingtoned busy widows and passed the time
Recounting the folklore gossip lifeblood of the tribe
Our forebears fought for better things for us
Their promised land a more disconnected if better paid
Submission to mammon sophisticated us and our clones returned
Ever rushing slaves to consumption bereft of tribe rootless

Modernised commodified and organised
Where before neighbours heard and walked casually
But purposefully to that drum that was the birthright
Of those who knew no other than belonging
For whom relationships were the only certainty
Who drank the knowledge of respect reciprocity and real tough uncompromising love
At resourceful and tenacious mother's teats
Who are no more – more's the pity!

This poem obviously has its origins in my experience but was inspired by much more contemporary events. Hospice volunteers who spent time visiting and befriending lonely and frightened terminally ill people observed that very often, after the demise of one of these folk, they would go to what they imagined would be a sadly ill-attended funeral only to find a very large gathering of apparently grieving friends and relatives.

It begs a very pertinent question. If people can only benefit from our love and care in vivo what is it about our society that gets in the way of us caring for each other with the passion we all merit?

In the last edition of his memoir, Hitch 22, Christopher Hitchens, in his final illness with death pretty much a certainty observes, "Another element of my memoir – the stupendous importance of love, friendship and solidarity – has been made immensely more vivid to me by recent experience. I can't hope to convey the full effect of the embraces and avowals but I can perhaps offer a crumb of counsel. If there is anybody known to you who might benefit from a letter or a visit ***do not on any account*** *postpone the writing or the making of it. The difference made will almost certainly be more than you have calculated."*

A place for Rose

Some years ago a colleague and I undertook a review of advocacy services for a Welsh Local Authority. As part of our review we interviewed numbers of people with disabilities who might have cause to seek help from advocacy agencies. In the course of this I met Rose. I met her one morning with four other people who attended the same Day Centre. Rose arrived in her catering uniform. She was, I was left in no doubt, a key member of the Centre's kitchen team.

To start the session I asked participants to introduce themselves, saying whatever they would like to share about their lives. When it came to Rose's turn she told us that she lived in a small ex-mining community with her Mum who was getting on and, these days, often unwell. Rose's sister lived a couple of doors away with her family and kept a general eye on Rose and her Mum but, it transpired that Rose, in reality, was doing most of the caring for Mum calling on help also from friends and neighbours when she needed. Rose told us that she was a lifelong member of the local chapel and miners' welfare and, if Mum hadn't been able to get out for cash, could get meals from the local takeaway and provisions from village shops on the slate. When asked about her social life there seemed to be barely a day in the week that did not involve a club, group, choir or event. And life at home seemed to involve a succession of visitors with the kettle always bubbling.

One of the other participants interjected with a question that I might have had difficulty in posing. "What will happen when your Mum dies?", he asked.
Rose was very matter of fact in her reply. "It's discussed at my reviews. When the time comes there will be a place for me in a Group Home".
"Are there Group Homes in your village?" immediately grabbed my tongue.
"No she said; I'll have to go where there's a vacancy."
"How do you feel about that?"

"Worried and sad – I've lived in the village all my life."
"Does your Social Worker know how you feel?"
"Yes, but he says that I shan't be allowed to have the tenancy if I'm on my own. He thinks I'll be better off in a Group Home and will have what I'm entitled to."

The group got very animated about this and spent the next half hour generating lots of possibilities regarding what could be done to ensure that Rose could remain in her community for the rest of her days. It did not take them long to come up with surefire tactics to get Rose the outcome she wanted.

That afternoon was spent with local Social Workers. During our discussions I anonymised Rose's circumstances and awaited their reaction. "Rose is very lucky to live in this authority", they said, "her situation will have been recognised at review and plans made to ensure that, when the time comes, she has priority for a Group Home place".

"But what if she wants to stay in her own home in her lifelong community?" I said.

"That's not how things are done here", they replied. "She wouldn't be allowed to keep the tenancy."

There's a place for Rose (A parody)
There's a place for Rose
A special place for Rose
Far from people she knows who care
At a price the State will bear

There's no scope for Rose
And little hope for Rose
Banished off to a vacancy
All procedurally

There's folk
Back there
Who know how Rosie is feeling
Know that she won't be revealing
Her loss
The cost

There's a place for Rose
Safeguarded place for Rose
In the car and we'll take you there
Pretty curtains and staff to care
Not here
With love
Somewhere

I'm Ray – an expert on institutions

Can you suspend your disbelief for a few minutes? I'm Ray, I died a couple of years ago, but I'd still like to tell you my story.

I was born in the early 1930's and at some point during the Second World War my Mum and Dad had me put away in Botley's Park because they couldn't cope with me. I spent the rest of my life in institutions – in psychiatric as well as mental handicap hospitals – until Borocourt Hospital was closed in 1992.

I had spent most of those years in locked or refractory wards. They are scary places where I never felt safe, where my constant preoccupation was on trying to get to stay safe. I was abused, physically and sexually, by other inmates. I was often forcibly restrained by staff, some of whom punched and kicked me, and I was sexually exploited by a staff member over a number of years. I soon learned that complaining was pointless.

When I'm anxious and frightened I try to run away. I ran away often when I was younger but - with nowhere to go and no money, food or shelter - I inevitably end up caught and locked in again somewhere, always with people who terrified me and with nurses who usually couldn't see how panic-stricken I was.

When I'm anxious and trapped something drives me to hurt myself. For some reason I find that hurting myself reduces my anxiety; makes me happier. I don't know why but pain inflicted on my private parts used to be particularly effective – and it made me sexually excited as well. I would find things – pencils, wire coat hangers, sticks, and the like – that I could push up my bottom or into my urethra. Once I determined to do away with myself by putting a plastic bag over my head. That, I found, was an experience that I enjoyed, so, instead of killing myself, I found myself hiding plastic bags about the place so that I could do it more.

But, in a locked ward there is little privacy. When they don't know where you are they come looking for you. And, when I was frequently found hurting myself in these ways, they rushed to stop me and, in restraining me, frightened me and often hurt me more. I lived in a vicious circle, a living hell, and became more and more feral and solitary. Staff feared me, not because I would hurt them, but because I disgusted them. This made me all the more vulnerable and subject to arbitrary treatment. When Borocourt closed the ward staff described me as the most challenging and inhuman person they had ever met.

With no provider agencies, it appeared, coming forward with viable proposals for the support of people like me, the people who had planned and led the closure of the hospital were asked to help and they set me up in a nice suburban house which I shared with two ladies who were about the same age as me who were said to have mental health problems. I helped to choose the house and the two ladies and I had the opportunity to meet each other a few times before we were asked whether we would be prepared to try living together. They said that no-one could be sure whether or not it would work out but would I like to give it a go? I had met and liked Nicola, who was to manage the staff, so I said yes although I was a bit flummoxed at being asked.

The move made me very anxious and so I resorted to hurting myself in my usual ways, sometimes barricading myself in my bedroom or a lavatory. This clearly upset Nicola and the staff, and sometimes they were so worried that they forced their way in to make sure that I was safe, but I was never restrained or kicked and punched. Instead they seemed intent on keeping things low key, calm. And, instead of ignoring me most of the time, they involved me in things – keeping house, preparing meals, doing the garden and meeting the neighbours. It wasn't long before I had a bit of a job looking after an elderly lady's garden and Janet had helped me learn how to cook a roast dinner so that, on Sunday mornings, the kitchen was mine.

So, after a couple of years in Tilehurst, I was beginning to enjoy life. I was a lot less anxious and, while I still had my moments (as Nicola used to say), they were much less frequent and intense. I had quite a social life and was secure amongst people who liked me. It went on like this for more than eight years. Nicola had married and moved to Wales where she soon had a family and I was an 'uncle' and god-parent. I used to visit, travelling alone on the coach. Justin, who had been there from the start, was now the manager and Nicola had offered to be my advocate. I was now into my 70's and I started have pain in my hip. One day the pain was excruciating and I was rushed into hospital where, to everyone's surprise, hip replacement surgery took place within days.

Then my life changed dramatically. After the surgery I couldn't wait to go home but they would not let me. A Hospital Social Worker came to see me and told me that she would sort out a place in an old people's home for me because I couldn't go back to Tilehurst because I wouldn't manage the stairs. I was very stressed and upset. Justin offered to convert a living room for me so that I would have a downstairs room but Social Services said he couldn't because that would affect the ladies I lived with. They said they were happy to have lounge upstairs but they would not listen. They said it was about rules and contracts. I thought that this was my home but it wasn't.

I was taken to the old people's home in an ambulance strapped into a wheelchair. I was scratched and bruised during the move and very distressed. Within hours the home decided that I could not be coped with, doctors were called, and I found myself sedated on the way to the Psychiatric Hospital. There were lots of meetings with Justin and his bosses insisting that the 'system' had clumsily caused my problems while clever professionals only wanted to talk about me being a risk to myself and others. Nicola raced up from Wales and told them about my life but they knew best. Meanwhile I had become incontinent and was refusing to eat. After a bust up they shut me in a seclusion room. I set a fire.

I was quickly moved to a specialist service for people with challenging behaviours where I found staff who had found me disgusting during my years in Borocourt. Nicola and Justin say that, at that point, it was as if I had decided to end things. I engaged in incessant self-neglect and rages of self-injury and the specialists scratched their heads.

Meanwhile Justin's bosses were lobbying frantically – which is always difficult when the marketized care system repeatedly jumps to conclusions that every provider is primarily looking for business. They were with my MP when the call came through to say that, as all else had failed, would they be good enough to see if they could organise a supported living service for me. Meanwhile Nicola put me in her car and took me home to Wales to stay with her family until arrangements could be made. I was asked what I wanted and I said that if I couldn't go back to Tilehurst I would like a place of my own not too far away.

The local council was both the social services and housing authority, so we thought that it wouldn't be too hard for them to come up with some housing options. It was, despite the urgency they reckoned it could take two years. So, after more lobbying, it was agreed that somewhere could be found in the private letting market and that Social Services would fund the difference between my Housing Benefit entitlement and the market rent (One public institution – numerous disconnected funding silos?). A beautiful, modern, ground floor Thames-side two bedroom flat was my choice from the affordable options uncovered and a few days later I moved in after my service provider had kindly undertaken to guarantee the lease when the Council refused to.

It was strange at first as I'd never had a place of my own ever before. I moved all the furniture and equipment into my bedroom because, to begin with, I could not understand that the whole of the flat was mine. Eventually I adjusted and spent 7 happy years there prior to my death. For much of that time I lived quite independently with, compared to the rest of my life, surprising little help – just three or four hours a day at one point. During that time I wanted people to hear my story. So I made a film.

Dreaming of a life without professionals

As parents, we are very aware of how the outside world can judge our actions: as parents of a son who has Down's Syndrome we have experienced a world of extremes from being really well supported by people who have listened to our concerns, stresses and deep anguish to a system which has marginalised our views whilst undermining our right to demand the best for our son.

Twenty seven years ago we had a beautiful son, Andrew, our second born, who was diagnosed by the clinicians as having Down's Syndrome and subsequently a major heart defect. During those early years we experienced all the usual ups and downs of bringing up a family with the added involvement of specialist education and clinicians. We did however, build some strong relationships with education and health which enabled Andrew to experience the ordinary stuff which most children encounter whilst growing up whilst at the same time relating to and sometimes challenging a system which can sometimes feel very punishing. Thinking back now it was the professionals who really listened to us who we related to best and gave us the strength to challenge when things were not so good. Andrew was a happy child, in the main, and because his schooling was local to his home he has managed to keep friends over many years.

Things started to get more challenging for us when, at the age of 21 Andrew parted company with the formal education system and became a full time "client" of the social care system. We had always wanted Andrew to be more independent and to experience the things his brother experiences so when an opportunity arose for Andrew to move into a supported living home sharing with 3 other people he took it. The first few months seemed good and then we started to notice some major issues which negatively impacted on Andrew's health and emotional wellbeing. Without going into much detail, it became quickly apparent that all was not well in the house where Andrew was living and the "care provider" was not being totally honest with us. So, when we found out that this was not working and challenged the provider, the situation went from bad to worse and Andrew ended up back at home with us. Needless to say, we were also not very impressed with the support we had from the Social Work service. After Andrew had been at home for a while we were told about the development of a supported living home which was very local to us and there would be really comprehensive compatibility process to ensure the three people, whose names had been put forward, would want to live together. At around this time Andrew health was also suffering and he ended up going into hospital for very serious heart surgery which kept him in hospital for a long time, but we thought that this new house would give Andrew something to look forward to after the operation and the rehabilitation. Although the process was fraught with difficulties and our relationship with the social work senior authorities was beginning to suffer, Andrew moved into his new home in September 2009. At that time, we had a new social Worker who convinced us that it would be a good idea to have an Individual Budget. Even though it was a relatively straight forward process to engage the new care provider, the other two people Andrew was going to share with didn't want to have the additional responsibility of taking this route. Because of the complexity of Andrew's care, including all the medication and other health related interventions we decided to engage a Support Broker using our Individual Budget to see if that would help us stay in control.

This new arrangement appeared to work for the first few months and then we noticed that Andrew's behaviour was changing and he was losing a lot of motivation. The Support Broker helped us with talking to the care provider and we became involved in monitoring the situation which didn't appear to be improving. The care provider then decided to withdraw their services from the home and we never knew the exact reason why they decided to go. A new provider was appointed with our involvement and everything started to improve until again, we started to be a little concerned about some of the staff and with Andrew's overall motivation. The leader from the Care Provider company, who we trusted most, then decided she didn't want any involvement with us and it became quickly apparent we were being marginalised in relation to our son's care. We then began to notice a wasting of resources by the care provider like staff being on duty when all the people in the house were at college: this was reinforced by the lack of hospitality within the home and Andrew's sometime reluctance to engage with opportunities not wanting to go back to his home after staying with us. Eventually we found out about a number of serious incidents within the home which had put Andrew at risk, so he came back to the family home once again.

This was the turning point for us as we realised that the one thing we can be sure of is if you engage an agency to care for your loved one, they will, at some point, let you down. The providers we had used were, in our opinion, motivated by profit and did not want to engage the important relationships which Andrew has in his life. Our Support Broker convinced us that a fresh approach was needed and we sat down over the next few months working out with Andrew the best way forward. Because Andrew already had an Individual Budget we were confident, with the support of our Broker we could start to be more creative and arrange the fresh start without care providers or agencies. It was interesting to note that the social work service were rather cynical about our ability to do this within the allocated monies. As it turned out, it was the best move we could have ever made. We planned with Andrew and he clearly wanted to live somewhere close to us in his own home, and not sharing with someone who also had a disability. We found a property locally and persuaded the landlord and agent that having Andrew as a tenant would be safe and secure because of his now very strong network of support. It took a while but eventually we found some people Andrew liked to share his home on a "Home-share" basis. This meant that Andrew had someone around overnight, which he needs because of his health issues, and they would offer some support in exchange for rent free accommodation. The support Broker helped us identify the support which was already available as part of Andrew's network and then we recruited a staff team to deliver all the support he requires. It was and is a fairly loose arrangement which has taken a little time to feel confident with, but it is also very adaptable to Andrew's ever changing lifestyle. The real benefits of taking this approach has been the amazing difference it has made to what Andrew now does on a day to day basis, his connections with his community, the self esteem gained from having a house which he now knows is his home and the opportunities that have arisen due to having a vibrant network of family, friends and paid staff. Andrew now has his own small business which builds on skills he learnt at college and now includes some of his friends and he very recently won an “It’s Your Neighbourhood” award for the local Britain in Bloom Association because of his (and a group of friends) work rejuvenating and maintaining a piece of land for all the community to enjoy. He has a full life and is fitter than he has been for many years, which is a great relief to the whole family. Because of the work Andrew does in the community and the network of friends support there are now plans to start a Time Bank so the wider community can be involved and see that our son and his friends can contribute and they can also benefit from a strong and vibrant community.

Life still throws up challenges and Andrew sometimes has bad days, just like the rest of us, but now we are confident that these challenges will be resolved without the full force of a social work system trying to put things right, but somehow always managing to create more problems and alienate us in the process.

Andrew's Good Life is now assured and we can relax a little!

Sheila & Euan Forsythe
Colin Campbell

Little Loner

Child, how I pondered on your gaze of stone,
your mute rejection of my rash embrace,
the iron will with which you stayed alone,
the puzzlement that froze your angel face.
Your loveless ordering and dumb control
willed me to dredge that hidden quality
from deep dark fathoms unknown to my soul
that piece by piece would build the better me.
And then one day you graced me with your smile
and warmly sought the comfort of my hand
as if to bid me stay and share awhile
your secret fears about the future and
how we two could take on all that life sends
if we walked on together as good friends.

MAKING COMETS OF LITTLE STARS

This story tells of some milestones of my relationship with my son Gareth on our road to our encounter with LivesthroughFriends. It could be a grim story, a funny story, a frightening story or one of devastating disappointments. I have opted to tell you the most useful story that can be told in the space allocated to me. It took place against a backcloth that included all those negatives mentioned above, but focuses on approaches that, like LivesthroughFriends, yielded positive results. It is actually a collection of six disparate stories that each illustrates four fundamental principles that seem to be embodies in the LivesthroughFriends approach.

The first story is about Gareth's attention span. At three he seldom stayed with any activity for more than a minute at best. At kindergarten the sandpit was his favourite, but after a little over a minute he would move off to spend a few seconds each on the other activities. It was obvious that his learning was being impaired and that something needed to be done.

With the help of a colleague in the Psychology Department at Cardiff University, a shaping program was devised, which I could administer. It involved rewarding Gareth with a smarty each time his attention to a task exceeded a predetermined baseline. The bar was ruthlessly raised as expedient and the results were formidable. Within weeks, Gareth could stay with any task for twenty five minutes, allowing him a good chance of gaining some useful skills.

The second story is about tongue drill. At five Gareth had no speech, but a committed educational psychologist used her skills, knowledge, guile and influence to wangle Gareth into contact with the most competent speech therapist in Wales. She said there was no guarantee that Gareth would ever acquire speech, and pointed out that toddlers acquiring speech subject their tongues to some spectacular exercises as they imitate the sounds produced by their parents, siblings, teachers and peers. The tongues of toddlers who do not acquire speech at the normal time miss out on this. When they later acquire speech, they have impediments due the seizing up of the tongue's musculature.

Her answer was tongue drill. She taught us to stand Gareth on a stool before a mirror. The tip of his nose, his cheeks and chin were dabbed with chocolate spread (which Gareth loved), and he was instructed to lick it off. This he did with great enthusiasm, manipulating and stretching his tongue in the process. Chocolate spread was reserved for this activity only, and Gareth would voluntarily present us with his stool and demand his tongue drill. Some years later Gareth did acquire speech, and this simple technique ensured that he produced perfect sounds. At infants' school, our dedicated psychologist enabled enthusiastic teachers to arm Gareth with a useful vocabulary, and this brings us to the third story.

The problem was that Gareth would only use speech to suit himself, usually one word at a time to get something he wanted. He had little truck with social chit-chat, so the next trick was to systematically expose Gareth to sentence structures, taking the process outside the confines of school. Our psychologist equipped us with flash cards designed to help us focus Gareth's attention on how language is used to describe a range of situations. These could be generalised to real situations, and we became adept at grabbing the opportunity of asking Gareth ' What is so-and-so doing?' eliciting the reply 'So-and-so is shaving/peeling potatoes/ reading/'washing etc. etc. etc.' At six, Gareth's vocabulary consisted of no more than twelve isolated words. At seven he would surprise us with remarkably complex structures, albeit in characteristic monotones.

Story number four concerns some of Gareth's post-infant achievements. Our ruthlessly committed educational psychologist had convinced the local education authority of the cost-effectiveness of keeping Gareth out of the residential setting that had been ear-marked for him. Staffing changes to a unit in a mainstream junior school enabled him to maintain contact with his non-disabled peers. To extend this outside his school life he joined the local Wolf Cub Pack. This was not without some degree of pain and poignancy as Gareth struggled to accommodate this new and challenging experience. The key to his remarkable success in gaining many badges as well as the heartfelt affection of the rest of the pack was the commitment of the two young men who ran the pack. They recognised Gareth's dogged willingness to learn and rose strongly to this fresh challenge. They had helped Gareth become a team-player, and when the summer play-scheme season came, Gareth declined the opportunity offered by the Special Needs segregated scheme and went, to the local mainstream scheme where everyone enjoyed Gareth's input.

The fifth story concerns Gareth's integration (again via our committed psychologist) into his local Comp. This was a grand success, resulting in good exam results, a congratulatory letter from the governors and a literate, numerate Gareth emerging onto adulthood's stage. Thus far my story must read like a blazing comet searing across a starlit sky. In fact the background sky had contained its fair share of darkness, and it now began to close in on Gareth's life. Buoyed up by the modern bright expectations encouraged by the All Wales Strategy, we had always expected Gareth to get a job and earn his living. Not so easy. It took three years with a supported employment scheme to get a part-time job in a sheltered workshop. Less than two years later the local authority withdrew its financial support and the factory closed. Despite almost superhuman efforts on his part, Gareth has never worked for pay since.

Thus, our sixth story involves five years of work-placements, interviews and pressure from DWP staff. Input from Social Services was limited to some segregated work experience and his annual Individual Plan Review, where his aim of getting paid employment was duly recorded. Combined with the loneliness and isolation his disability brings, the experience began to take its toll and Gareth's health deteriorated rapidly. We were close to despair until one of Gareth's old contacts enthusiastically introduced us to LivesthroughFriends. Things began to be turned around as Bob spent time with Gareth and brokered a deal with the local authority using Direct Payments. Gareth employed a network facilitator and a circle of supportive contacts was built up. The outcomes have been dynamic. Gareth's health, confidence and enthusiasm have been restored and he is currently waiting for the outcome of his most recent job interview. For the first time since 2003, his long term emotional future looks secure. The comet is raising its head.

The six success stories seem to share four fundamental principles: recognition of problems, supportive empowerment, normality of situation, and individual focus. In every situation the specific problem faced by Gareth was identified and recognised. It was obviously no good just treating him like anybody else; something special was done. Each strategy was delivered by ordinary people like parents, teachers, Akelas, play leaders, friends and neighbours, who were empowered to help Gareth improve his situation. The approaches may have been specialist in design, but were always administered by people found naturally in Gareth's environment. Moreover, generally speaking the support took place in ordinary situations, not in segregated settings. Most important, in every case the focus was on Gareth, not on a group identified by a label. There is little point in focusing on the darkness. The trick is to identify little stars that can become comets. LivesthroughFriends is good at this.

Ken Davies November 2012

When Nothing is Your Meaning

Penny is Thirty years old today - I am invited, by her(as a friend), to a review arranged by her Social Worker. There are two people from the private care provider also in attendance: the senior manager of the care company and Penny's "Care Co-ordinator". The meeting starts with the Manager producing a large cake from her bag which she tells Penny is for her birthday. We all have a piece of cake, then the meeting begins.

The review is to focus on the current problems in Penny's life and starts by attempting to go through an "Action" list from the previous meeting. We get to point three of the actions on the list with none of them yet achieved when Penny launches into a verbal assault on the manager around how she does not want to be seen as second best to other people the care agency supports: she relays a story, which is confirmed by the manager, of not receiving support when one of the other "clients", who require 24 hour support, needs help. The Manager clarifies, apologetically, that when there are staff shortages she does have to prioritise the people under her care who have the greater need. Penny is very angry and distressed about this. Penny then launches into a further verbal assault which, in my opinion, also describes what she really wants from her support.

What Penny wants, is an opportunity to employ her <u>own</u> staff team using a Personal Budget and start to do the things that she really wants to do. After all, it can't be any worse than what is currently happening. The Social Worker explains to everybody that Penny would need a lot of support to administer the Personal budget and this is not currently available locally. The care co-ordinator expanded on this by saying that it is better to have a specific care provider who takes away all the worry of managing the care and it is probably cheaper because you would have to pay someone to help manage a Personal Budget. This plays into Penny's known anxiety around money worries. I try and intervene (knowing it's too late) by saying that there are alternatives and support can be made available if all the people at the meeting were willing to support the approach. By this time Penny was getting very upset and tearful which provoked an accusation from the care co-ordinator that I was over complicating things for Penny and not being very helpful. At this point Penny had to be escorted from the room to a separate area in order to calm down and be appeased. The Social worker followed Penny out of the room and the Manager decided she was probably contributing to the distress and made her apologies, leaving, taking the cake with her!.

I have to confess, that this sort of scene, at a meeting, has been common place in the ten years I have known Penny. The outcome is always the same; there are, I think, well meaning people (different each time) who are part of a care delivery system which is convinced that the same sort of support, which has never really worked for Penny, will somehow, work this time. Over the years that I have known Penny I have had to moderate what I say as sometimes it can have a negative impact on Penny after the meeting when she starts to feel punished by the paid support in her life. This can result in making things more restrictive and stressful in the short term. In this never ending cycle of events we always seem to end up in the same position with Penny knowing that she doesn't want the sort of support she is getting, but doesn't want to leave the only daily relationships (all paid) which touch her ever changing world.

Penny has a label of Asperger's Syndrome and it has to be said, has always had a difficult time managing what day to day life throws up, which in my experience is not unusual for someone who has a chaotic upbringing and has Asperger's Syndrome. This has, over the years, consistently led to extreme times when everything breaks down and Penny runs away and manages to find the worst sort of company, which puts her at risk. Because of this, I have always walked a fine line in Penny's life offering specific support when requested and being very cautious with my communication with professionals. For example, I have helped Penny start to put a relationship Network together only to see it undermined by paid staff who have, at best, not seen the value of such a network and at worst have deliberately sabotaged the network. I don't necessarily see the paid people who are around Penny as being bad people, but I just think they are so locked into their own systems and ways of working that they are unable to visualise what a good life would look like for Penny. Unfortunately, Penny, due to her personal challenges, will sometimes reinforce this approach by using their language and approaches to reinforce her own lack of meaning and control and the her deep rooted feelings of emptiness, which unfortunately, is all too real for her.

At the end of the meeting with only 3 points of the "Action" list completed, I am told that Penny is being evicted from her flat in three months because the care provider is selling off all their properties. The care provider has been bought out at least three times in the last three years and, I guess, the latest owner sees more value in the properties than the people. This means another crisis looming and the same cycle of lack of control and anger which Penny will manage in her own inimitable way. Slightly stunned by this I bring up the subject, which Penny had highlighted too me, around her desire to visit her Mum, who lives 90 miles away, more regularly. I had discussed this with Penny prior to the meeting so I suggested that Penny might like to be supported to go to the local volunteer bureau and see if they could help recruit a volunteer to support Penny with visiting her Mum once a month. The Social worker immediately gave a counter suggestion of going back to the Local Authority resource panel to ask for more money so the care agency could support Penny with an extra visit. The immediate response from the care co-ordinator was to say to Penny that this would mean she could choose her favourite member of staff to take her: Penny is excited and happy about this and of course agreed to this course of "Action". I'm deflated and of course support Penny with this decision whilst mentally adding up all the past decisions which have never been followed up. My mind then drifts to how long it will be before I get the inevitable phone call from Penny and we have the same distressing conversation again.

Colin Campbell, October 2012

"Billie Placement" – A Meeting (1) An Everyday Story of Complex Folk

It was a couple of weeks to Christmas when a domiciliary care manager contacted me to see whether we could help Sandra and her 60 year old sister, Billie. The care agency had supported Sandra in caring for her husband during his last illness. On the very day of his death they observed the strong and resourceful Sandra they know inevitably crumpling under pressure from a number of often well-meaning professionals to make what she perceived to be yet another arbitrary decision about the next in a litany of failed placements for Billie.

Billie has a learning disability, has been in the care system since her mid-twenties, seems to have rubbed along quite contently during her thirties when she was supported in a small family run setting which eventually was sold as the result of a marital breakup, and subsequently in another setting in a seaside town until the onset of, initially undiagnosed, early onset dementia saw her insidiously recategorized as 'challenging'.

Be under no illusion, supporting – that is being with and caring for Billie – is demanding work that demands resilience, resourcefulness, and lots of tolerance and tenacity. Those who know and love her are clear that no-one should spend more than four hours per shift with her. She is described in terms that are classically associated with dementia. She's restless, inherently confused and unpredictable, often disconnected from the expected rhythms of daily life, and, given the chaos of her later life, post-traumatically stressed. Physical problems, with swallowing and the complications of a brain injury and pelvic fracture resulting from one or more falls, complicate the picture further.

As a result of her 'challenging' label Billie had made her way to a now very notorious private 'hospital' where, despite all than transpired subsequently she seems to have not been badly treated. There a dementia diagnosis was confirmed and, very appropriately, Billie was enabled to move out to a specialist dementia service where she had seemed much less agitated, more contented and settled. However this was not a long term arrangement and learning disability commissioners sought out another 'final solution' and Billie was placed with a high cost support package in a new supported living setting out of county and some 40 plus miles away from her sister. It was here that the falls had occurred that had left Billie in hospital being investigated primarily for stroke in the first instance and where, eventually, her pelvic fracture and brain injury were identified. Meanwhile the service served notice on Billie, who was superficially and in accordance with good practice a secure tenant who could have chosen to continue to live in her home and secure care and support from another source. It seems that this supposed protection was not...

Hence, within a day (to their credit) of Sandra's request for an urgent meeting to discuss Billie's situation, we (Sandra, Billie's advocate, and I) met with 5 commissioners just 3 working days before Billie was de facto scheduled to be discharged from hospital and admitted to a medium secure, medical model, challenging behaviour assessment and treatment service in Wales. We arrived with clear goals; to mitigate the impact of the decision that had already been taken on Billie, ensuring that this placement would be of an interim nature and that henceforward a committed programme would be enacted to secure a truly bespoke and sustainable support arrangement for her.

I had met Sandra with Billie's advocate for the first time the previous day following telephone conversations during which I had both secured a superficial grasp of Billie's story, explained LivesthroughFriends approach to intensive support brokerage or - as we increasingly prefer to describe it – supporting people and families to self-direct, and satisfied myself that Sandra shared our critique of monetised social care and understood her central role in doing things differently.

Our commissioning hosts received us warmly, professionally, and most importantly openly. There was no defensive posturing in defence of the de facto decision. We had asked for the top person to be present and she chaired the meeting skilfully, listening actively and seeking common ground. It seemed that an apologetic "Maggie" posture was genuinely presented. "It's far from perfect but we've investigated 30 possible placements that might provide a match for her needs, and only two can help of which one has a much better regulator's report than the other, so there's really no alternative", was the gist of their explanation.

I offered an alternative perspective, suggesting that the obsession with seeking solutions by fitting folk like Billie into 'placements' was largely the source of her difficulties and that both much better outcomes and improved economy will usually be achieved by the incremental and iterative development of personalised arrangements. And I described Sandra's interest in taking a lead, with support, in directing and coordinating her sister's support.

First up it seemed like the nub of my observations had been unheard or expressed in some foreign tongue (I do have a West Country burr, but we were in the West Country!). The need to develop a market of providers to this work was mooted and then amended with the observation that it existed with respect to less complex people. As this unfolded I felt sure that what they saw as self-direction I saw as monetised social care open as usual.

I shared my experiences of reading the relevant minutes and correspondence relating to Billie's situation and conversations with Sandra and professionals who knew her well and observed that, without her sister's perspectives, I, having never met Billie, would have no idea of who she is. It seemed to me that, to the professional world, Billie is simply a bundle of pathologies. I asked about the service specification and whether that had much to say about Billie the person? Having elicited little from this enquiry I continued to suggest that, based on what I had heard, Billie is a frightened, vulnerable, medically frail and complex lady with dementia who is desperate for stability, continuity, love and sensitive care.

Evidence from all the sources suggested that Billie had as good as flourished during her stay in a dementia service. She had gone there when the Consultant Psychiatrist at the soon to be disgraced Medium Secure Hospital had diagnosed dementia and protested that she was inappropriately placed in a challenging behaviour setting. I shared my confusion about why, given the evidence, a known error was being repeated? I was told that lots of possible placements had been investigated but none were prepared to help Billie. I don't believe that any of the commissioners have any idea that it is possible and desirable to develop a network of providers that are prepared to learn with us to work creatively and iteratively with complex people. And experience tells me that there are plenty of aspirational and ethical leaders who are keen to work collaboratively. It's just that most commissioners don't have the knowledge, skills, confidence and practice credibility (and perhaps desire?) to come out from behind their bureaucratic and procedural shields.

Sandra was clear that the proposed but de facto placement in a medium secure setting should be explicitly viewed and contracted as a holding arrangement and that work on planning and delivering a bespoke domestic-style arrangement within which her sister would be a truly secure tenant should be commenced immediately. The health commissioner irritably responded by saying that she did not believe that this was not the basis upon which a long term placement had been negotiated with the provider. I reported that I had researched the proposed provider and that their website was clear that they provided specifically an assessment and treatment service with stays not usually exceeding 12 –15 months.

The social worker was despatched to ring the provider and returned confirming that a short contract was possible. Nonetheless commissioners expressed the hope that Billie would "settle" in this very inappropriate place. There was now no doubt that disposal alone was the driving motivation of the powerful professionals who control Billie's life.

Given Sandra's calmly expressed concerns about both the placement and the actual move it was agreed that another gathering would be quickly convened, just a week after Billie's move. Long term planning would start at that meeting...

Billie Placement – Another Meeting (2) "Pretending to be Working"

It's just 10 days later. Billie was transferred to the semi-secure challenging behaviour service from the General Hospital a week ago. She has, in addition to her apparent dementia - a fractured pelvis, dislocated shoulder, an open bedsore, swallowing difficulties, and has not been out of bed since she arrived. Her room is just big enough to accommodate her bed and two chairs for the staff who are continuously with her. There is no room for her personal recliner chair. Given Billie's known susceptibility to chest and urinary tract infections this seems a far from satisfactory situation. Commissioners have visited but seem to have not appreciated the implications of this regime.

Sandra has visited twice and is worried. Amongst a number of concerns she cites incredulity at the care provider's incompetence in managing her sister's swallowing problems. Billie cannot tolerate fluids. To maintain hydration Billie needs frequent small drinks, thickened to the consistency of jelly, and caringly spoon-fed. On a visit she had to intervene when a carer set out to fill a spouted feeding cup and simply give that to Billie. It took her some time to effectively 'train' the support workers in this basic aspect of her sister's care; this after carers from her previous supported living placement had spent 4 days modelling the necessary basic care programme. The commissioners undertook to take this up on their next visit and seemed not able or willing to draw the conclusion that, if such a key element of Billie's care was unaddressed, there may be many equally important areas to worry over. The meeting's chair assumed a "Violet Elizabeth" pout when I quietly asserted that the Care Plan should be acquired; then acerbically instructed the note-taker to add this to the list. This protocol was followed on each occasion, as there were several when Sandra, Billie's advocate, or I reminder her about the bare essentials of the commissioner's role.

The meeting had started as it was to continue. The Lead Commissioner who had facilitated a real dialogue in the previous meeting was not present. We were presented with an agenda to agree – hard not to when it is done this way – which made no reference to planning a proper solution to Billie's situation and ended with agreeing a date for another meeting 3 months hence. We were advised that the Commissioner had signed a contract for 12 months with the Provider which meant, as I felt it, a non-judicial 12 month sentence to lovelessness for Billie. We were being 'managed'. They had decided that there was little point initiating real planning for Billie's future while so many medical issues were unresolved and commissioned further investigations through and by the provider. It seemed to me to be just more evidence of health professionals redefining Billie in their silos of perceived but not immediately evident competence. Billie had been deemed fit for discharge by a hospital. What she needed was loving and consistent care to manage her frailties and, where possible, support her recovery. Instead she was being and continues to be unforgivably and disgracefully categorized on the basis of historical labels, a system that responds to baskets of pathologies and has only a politically correct appreciation of personalisation, and is absolutely subservient to providers who, in reality, control what amounts to a perverse slave market.

Despite requests we have not been shown, nor less contributed to, any service specification for Billie. If such exists I have no doubt that this will amount to a description of Billie's often miserable history and an over-emphasised declamation of her needs and deficits. I would lay odds that there will be no attempt at a vision of what will need to be attempted, let alone achieved, in order that Billie has the prospect of a life worth living. In the final analysis one has to draw the conclusion that such professionals have somehow insulated themselves from an emotional response to the wrongness of Billie's situation. It seems to me that they have rationalised their own impotence and incompetence by internalising the notion that there is no alternative. When confronted with those who assert that there are many alternatives they, instead of smiling and asking to be shown other ways, see this as a slight on their standing and reputations. And then the system offers them a host of hooks to hang this particular hat upon. Hooks associated with procurement rules, risk assessment, professional compliance, institutional inertia, contradictory policies – the list is probably endless!

I've come to view Billie's story as, "An Everyday Story of Complex Folk". If you have complex needs there is every chance that you and your life will end up defined by your pathologies and deficits – the stuff that expert professionals claim to be good at sorting out. And it's very likely that, unless you have a Sandra in your life, it will be a rare day that anyone will see the real you and your potential for a worthwhile life. And even then family and friends have to be really organised and tenacious in order to ensure that your humanity is truly appreciated and addressed. It would be nice to be optimistic that professions and institutions will one day really grasp and run with the fundamental non-negotiables of personalisation – but I'm not. Experience has taught me that, for complex folk to have the lives they deserve, people who love them must be in control.

One of the professionals in the meeting drank from a mug emblazoned with the logo,

"Just pretending that I'm working".

Through my frustrated and largely unexpressed anger burst a paradoxical giggle. Unwittingly this expressed the real state of social care commissioning in this place. I'm not suggesting that folk we met are lazy. But they are charging around with lots of "noise and thunder, signifying nothing"; knowing that they are going through the motions and that they are engaged in securing a succession of inappropriate and terminally failing 'placements'. They know that what they do is not working but, like hamsters on a wheel, they keep on doing it. So, when push comes to shove, they are "just pretending that they are working". I can't escape the thought that this is just the same for all the policy nerds for whom none of the foregoing is new or shocking. Perhaps they are in the same rudderless boat – unable to look beyond the institutional and professional knowledge and systems that some might call their comfort zone?

REVIEWING YOUR GOOD LIFE

When people receive public money there are always strings attached: it's called being accountable for the public purse!. A Personal budget is no different. Local Authorities have different interpretations on how personal budgets should be used although the guiding principle should be that the monies allocated should be used to legally deliver the agreed outcomes for the individual who requires the support. So, you probably couldn't use the money to buy someone else a holiday or use the money to gamble at the races! However, the spirit of Personal budgets should always encourage creative use, which should entail looking outside of what is traditionally available in order to build on what works for you as an individual, your unique aspirations and specific support requirements. I am aware, of course, that some Local Authorities may make specific rules around what the money should be spent on, which will limit the creativity I refer to: this however, does not, in my opinion, embrace the values and "spirit" of Personal Budgets and should, where possible, be challenged. Having said that, all Personal budgets are monitored in some way and one of those ways is the dreaded social work annual review. My view is that you should always try and take as much control of this process as possible and also use it as a way of celebrating the successes and to reinforce the strengths of the approach you are taking. Any challenges should always be highlighted, and preferably dealt with prior to the review process: this should be good practice in the eyes of all stakeholders.

Recently, I had a phone call from a Social worker asking for a date to undertake a review. I spoke to the person who's support was being reviewed and he, alongside his family, agreed that the best way of "reviewing" was to have a social gathering (a tea party) on a Sunday afternoon in which all the people important to the individual could be invited to come and be involved. At first the Social worker was slightly apprehensive about working on a Sunday and needed to check it out with his supervisors. His supervisors agreed, which led us to the next challenge of how the Social worker could gather the information he needed to feed the system (to tick all the Local authority boxes!) from a loosely structured gathering. The social worker shared all the Local Authority forms prior to the party and we all thought that a simple poster presentation of the individuals Good Life would easily demonstrate what was needed for the Social workers forms: the Social Worker would need to be creative around interpreting the information gathered, but it would be better than sitting around a table for two hours, feeling out of control. We agreed to work on four posters prior to the party which would demonstrate what had been happening over the last 12 months and to have another graphic poster which would be focussed on Imagining a Good Life, which could stimulate focussed discussion for all the family and friends coming to the tea party. There would also be a graffiti wall where people could offer ideas for the future and pledges of support (if required) to enhance the person's good life. See below.

MY GOOD LIFE

- **Sharing my home with someone I like (Home-share)**
- **Build up my micro-business**
- **Involving more people in my "Britain in Bloom" plot**
- **Spending time with my family and friends**
- **Going to the Gym twice a week and walking as much as possible (I need to stay as fit and healthy as possible)**
- **Continue my job (& socialising) at the Rugby club**
- **Having a full and varied social life, doing stuff which I look forward to and I'm passionate about**
- **Making more choices about what I do each week**
- **Co-ordinating my "supports" better so my Mum isn't as busy**
- **Be part of a new community Time Bank and involve my current friends and make new ones**

The afternoon was a great success with a number of the individuals' family and friends attending and contributing. The posters were left up for a week as other members of the network of friends and family had promised to pop in over the week because they couldn't make the party. One interesting outcome of the afternoon was the number of other families, who also had a caring responsibility, wanting to know more about how the outcomes on the posters were being so successfully delivered from having a Personal Budget. There was also some interesting conversations about the potential for expanding the network locally so a network of networks could be developed which could offer mutual support and more opportunities without referring back to the Local Authority all the time. One parent of a young man with learning disability thought about how much money was being wasted on his son with little positive outcomes and an increased level of stress and worry for him. He explained that, since his wife died, and he became the main carer of his son, the intensity of his relationship with his son was having a negative impact on them both and he was worried for the future. The Local Authority had arranged for a care provider to take his son out three times a week and this was inconsistent due to the company not being able to follow through on agreements and the restrictions on what they seemed able to do with his son. This parent was also persuaded to take a small Direct Payment which appeared to come with lots of restrictions around when it could be used and a Direct Payments support company who added to the stress due to their badly worded and intimidating correspondence and general incompetence. He had stuck with all these "support because he could not see any alternatives and his energy levels around doing anything about it were diminishing fast. He did however, say that it would be really nice if there was more practical mutual support: he went on to describe a potential scenario where a group of carers could come together and arrange breaks for their loved ones built around common interests. What he wanted was less pressure from so called professionals so he could take advantage of the benefits of having a Personal budget, but at this point he didn't really trust the Local Authority (or Direct Payments company) not to interfere and undermine any good work that could be done. This is a real indictment of the current situation within social care where on one hand the Local Authorities publicity and marketing machine is pushing "personalisation" yet the system appears to contradict and undermine the process at all stages due to a lack of trust and insight into how individuals' and community actually operate. It seemed to this carer that the system was not only driving the personalisation vehicle but was also building manned roadblocks to slow it down to a standstill. "In my experience too many managers and not enough leadership will always do this", he said.

Back to the tea party! Some interesting ideas came out of the afternoon which will contribute to the individuals' good life. I also think it was a great learning for the Social Worker in relation to the power of strong Relationship Networks and to the benefits of not having complex tick box approaches to reviewing peoples' lives. We've all had enough of meaningless meetings which only reinforce what we have always done and do not encourage looking at life through a new lens, as this is what will generate a new and interesting lan.

Getting Rhys to School – plus Tinker Tinker

It was a run-of-the-mill telephone enquiry. She wanted her team to be more creative, to respond more immediately and effectively to people, to make better use of all the resources available, and so on. Another of our clients had told her how effective our version of Go MAD training had been in her department. Could we do something similar for her and her people?

I widened the conversation. I like to know the context in which our interventions are set. Invariably folk don't have the time or money to invest in the full Monty so it is usually helpful to know which elements of the Go MAD framework should be prioritised in the context of the outcomes our customers want delivered. Usually this is arrived at by detailed discussion and challenge. I find it's preferable to work out how to deal with sacred cows and folk's 'ugly babies' in advance.

As our conversation unfolded it seemed that I was being asked to address something that, while effective and creative thinking would be part of the remedy, was far more cultural and institutionalised. For me, all the lights flashed on when she told me this story...

A woman, Sian, who (and this to me seems important) was already known to the team, had been in touch. She had been diagnosed with an untreatable condition and advised that she had, at best prognosis, only a short time to live. She enjoyed a robust family life with a much loved partner and a young son, Rhys. Her husband's work involved 10 hour shifts, starting at 6 every morning. This meant that on most school days he couldn't be around to walk young Rhys to and from school.

Sian was, it seems, pretty clear about how she wanted to manage the remaining days of her life and had organised accordingly. The one thing she had not managed to arrange was the apparently matter of fact practicalities of getting Rhys safely to school.

The 'adult' team Social Worker allocated the case – who knew Sian through support provided at an earlier stage in her illness – listened to Sian and advised her that she could not help but would refer the matter on to colleagues in Children & Families. The Social Worker was challenged over this by her supervisor – who suggested that it would not be too onerous a task to speak with neighbours, the school, and in due course parents of other children attending the same school. The Social Worker stuck to her guns. They "didn't do kids", there would be "safeguarding issues", and, as the supervisor saw it, the Social Worker was "not in her comfort zone" and "stuck in her silo". So the supervisor sought guidance from above (her boss) and was told unequivocally to refer on to children's services "to avoid repercussions".
This she did. Subsequently she found out that no-one in the Children's team had seen fit to sort out a sustainable, local and communal solution to Sian's request. Instead arrangements had been made for a domiciliary care company to provide someone to escort Rhys to and from school. "Of course, she said, this arrangement will cease as soon as Sian dies!"

In my naivety I imagined that this must be an aberration. It would not be like this anywhere else? So in the following days, as I conversed with social services friends in a number of authorities, I posed Sian's request and asked them what would transpire on their manor. Without exception they regretfully confessed that in their authority getting Rhys to school would be reduced to a commercial transaction.

So you won't be surprised to learn that while I offered to provide some experiential support brokerage training (that incorporates effective thinking elements) for the team I also stressed the importance of radically changing the systems and culture that causes allegedly intelligent professionals to behave irrationally. That is, my many decades in this work tell me, the ultimate commission.

Tinker, Tinker.

(An exercise in offending as many well-intentioned public servants as possible)

Give the people what they crave
Need not work and never save
Be their saviour yes I can
Tinker tinker Alderman

We can fix it in a jiffy
Though our plans are often iffy
Square the circle make it pat
Tinker tinker bureaucrat

I can make your every need
Prey to entrepreneurial greed
Marketize while you stay dormant
Tinker tinker in procurement

You've a platform sweet delight
Do what wins and not what's right
Celebrity you can't resist
Tinker tinker populist

Democracy as everyone knows
Is well and good as far as it goes
Takes leaders who can smell a rat
Tinker tinker autocrat

If you cannot do inspect
Set the rules demand respect
Ethics of an alligator
Tinker tinker regulator

We can't operate without
Rules that leave us free of doubt
No matter that they're rarely fair
Tinker tinker barrister

I'm an expert in my field
Power I wield can't be appealed
Stole your rights now rarely missed
Tinker tinker specialist

We have all annexed your lives
Occupied proceduralised
Big careers at your expense
Tinker tinker – God you're dense!

I speculate and fantasize
That we're all bigger than the lies
That make the State the first default
Tinker tinker... or revolt!

What Goes Round – Sometimes Comes Round Changed?

I was up at 5 and away at 6 this morning to catch a train to a meeting of leaders and thinkers who are passionate about putting citizens at the centre of welfare reform, responsible for and in control of their lives. I'd been up until nearly midnight preening the 'earthmoving' presentation I'd self-consciously decided to make and continued my preparations on the train, unconvinced of the coherence of my argument and anxious that my audience would be able to grasp the points I was so desperate to explain.

In the event I should not have worried. It was clear from the start that everyone at the gathering – folk who can boast exceptional against the odds achievements in practically demonstrating personalisation and self direction – was suffering from the same anxiety. How does one present inspiring stories and progressive ideas on expanding the contributing citizenship and inclusion of folk who depend upon welfare support in the face of the least sympathetic and, history may conclude, most dishonest and divisive domestic government for the best part of a century and a disempowered, meekly compliant, incompetent and dependent consumer culture?

Speakers seemed to have three main strategies. One was to rail at the iniquity and absurdity of the prevailing chaos in UK social care. The second was (I was one of these) to propose giving up on any hope of meaningful political and systemic change. (That is, unless and until a bottom-up cultural and societal revolution and renewal movement, applying the values and skills associated with communal interdependence, reciprocity and mutuality, might be re-ignited. And then proposing actions and strategies designed to spark and fan the flames.) The third was essentially to do both while clinging to a vague expectation that the essential goodness of the welfare state might eventually win through. Anger, disbelief and expressions of impotence clouded the thoughts of most practitioners and providers. Family members and those who primarily write and consult tended to home in on proposals and strategies that might be progressed without too much institutional support or even in the face of bureaucratic opposition or obfuscation.

I am probably making the day appear depressing and unproductive – it wasn't! When folk who share a strong and resolute value system, loyalty and commitments to flesh and blood people, and tenacious and creative personalities connect, listen well to each other, and strive for solutions; the room sparkles.

Commitments to action, to collaborations, to investigation and reflection, and to mutual support populated the plenary discussions. I and many others made our return journeys re-energised, powerful and humble.

What Goes Around...?

On the train home I experienced a sense of déjà vu. Politicians and institutional bureaucracies making bad, reactive and arbitrary decisions and demonstrating absolute mistrust of the British people is par for the course. The 'system's' inability to adopt Einstein's maxim that, "not everything that can be counted counts and not everything that counts can be counted" – or, in my construct, recognise that much of what really counts in our lives is relational and reciprocal and neither amenable to institutional command and control mechanisms nor to commodification by 'care' businesses (profit making or not!) – is hardly news either. The challenge doesn't seem to have changed a great deal – that being to demonstrate better ways to realise the values and principles we espouse, maintain our integrity, make a real difference if only for a few, and hope that others learn from and build upon our efforts.

But, in one way, it has. As time goes on, and generations succeed generations, the knowledge, skills and 'innateness' of familial and communal self-reliance, interdependence, and, as Paul Ginsborg puts it, "active and dissenting" participative democracy is giving way to outsourced 'care' and privatised disconnected 'plutocracy'. As a society we seem to becoming increasingly dependent upon and vulnerable to experts. Experts who identify gaps in the 'needs market', insist that only these with their talents can respond to these 'problems', and invite us to consume their remedies, their lobbying skills, their products and their excuses.

It strikes me that our addiction to dependent consumption is as self-defeating as successive governments' addictions to creating a short-term mirage of economic competence by stimulating domestic spending. First, like most if not all addictions, the outcomes achieved are quickly experienced as unsatisfying. In the case of social care we are left as unsatisfied when we all too often expect to experience care but find that we are simply a medium for the undertaking of specified tasks. And, second, I conclude that, as our consumer society falls prey to more and deeper economic and environmental stresses, the State will progressively shrink its welfare spending. Incompetent communities peopled by dependent and angry frustrated consumers seem to me to be a divisive and terrifying prospect.

Mr Cameron might do well to dwell on this and even to think the unthinkable. Could it be that the market has little or no place in how we ensure that we care for each other throughout our lives in the UK? Could it be that the real volunteers might be family, friends, neighbours and associates who share our interests and passions? Who would recoil at the term 'volunteer' in the context of their engagement with those they love and like – with whom they enjoy a relationship? Who would perhaps revel in the opportunity to engage far more in the joys and duties of mutual care and support, of community and involvement, if they were not distracted by being induced to work longer and harder in order to own more and better things they may not really need and to purchase the distractions and entertainments that they must surely need for their recreation? People aren't choosing to live this way. They are groomed for their role.

These insights blew away the Turneresque clouds of déjà vu. We have not been here before. We are on a road to an unpredictable destination. It might be sensible to retrace our steps or stop and give some thought to where we want to go?

SYSTEMS IN-ACTION

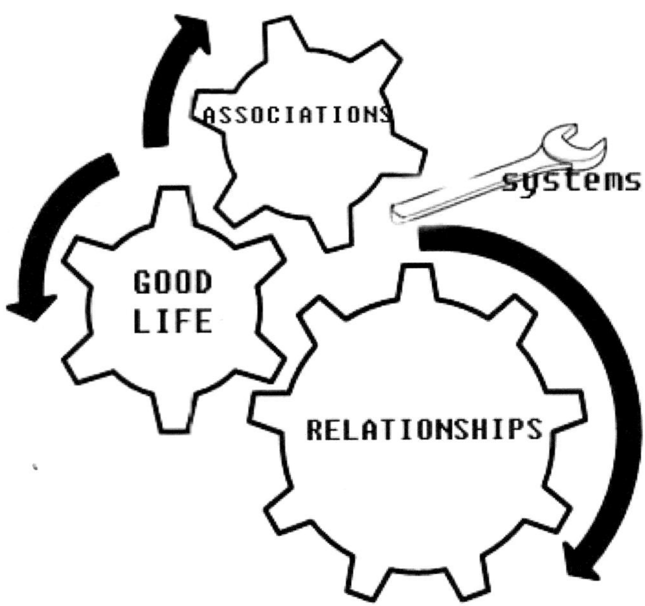

I had a telephone call today from someone who described, what I think, is a great example of the lunacy of our "social care" system. The woman was phoning me to talk through her situation and to ask about personal budgets. She told me her husband has Parkinson's disease and his condition had worsened over the past two years resulting in him now needing a wheel chair to get around and a higher level of day to day care. She had been having ongoing dialogue with the Local authority Social Worker and the Occupational Therapist service. This has resulted in a number of adaptations to the couple's property, including the provision of special bed, lifting/transferring aids etc. In addition her husband was assessed as "needing" 1/2 hour a day domiciliary care. She also told me that she struggles with the physical care tasks she has to undertake for her husband due to her own health problems and she was beginning to get very stressed due to the systems she was having to interact with. She described one of the reasons for the stress, which was focussed on the arrangements for the 1/2 hour daily domiciliary care. She then went on to relay how the care was arranged: Her husband was financially assessed and he qualified for financial help as his savings were below the higher threshold but above the lower threshold. The Local authority assessed that he would need to contribute £15.50 per hour for the care he received. The Local Authority "Care Manager" then directly contracted with a Domiciliary provider who then started sending a "carer" in to the family home every morning to help out. Over the past 18 months this has been causing stress because of the inconsistency of support and lack of continuity of "carers": for example, last week, five different "carers" visited over six days - one of the days they completely missed the visit. It quickly became apparent to me that this is only a small part of the story. At no point has any professional asked about her husband's life, what he does, what he would like to do, how often he sees friends, what other supports would help him retain and sustain good life? All the actions taken so far have reflected an institutional system, which appears unable to connect with the family's situation and then act accordingly. Don't get me wrong, they have addressed some of the very practical issues which will ease some of the pain of caring, however, no one has prioritised what really matters in respect of what really works well and the strengths of the individuals concerned, in the context of a community which they have lived for over thirty years. The Local Authority had merely followed a protocol which is not only counterproductive in relation to producing the required "quality of life" outcomes but is also financially inefficient. The reasoning behind invoicing someone for £15.50 per hour and then identifying and contracting with a domiciliary care provider who then invoices the Local authority does not appear like the best approach, especially as it doesn't deliver what is required. I also suspect, the domiciliary provider is paid less than £15.50 per hour which means there is no benefit financially to the individual being so narrowly assessed by a Care Manager and engaging the Local Authority in the first place. So, where was the common sense in all these transactions?

The sad fact about this situation is that more resources will end up being needed due to the processes created by a system which has forgotten why they exist. So, is there a better way? People tell me that in these situations the use of Personal Budgets will not help because the care hours needed does not warrant the resources associated with supporting the family to think creatively and find alternative solutions. I am convinced that this is not the case: Let's dream a little and go through the whole process in a slightly different way. Husband and wife have been living in their current home for thirty years and their lives are suddenly radically changed due to the husband having Parkinson's disease which leaves him requiring a wheelchair to get around and the need for significant levels of care to get through each day. The wife is struggling to cope and is physically and emotionally drained. A referral is made to the local social work department and an Occupational Therapist makes an initial assessment which addresses the adaptations and then a Social worker visits to have a conversation about additional support. The Social Worker recognises that the situation is desperate and additional help is required. The Social Worker asks "what does a good life look like for you both". They talk about all the things they used to do and all the friends they had, and their immediate family who have now moved out of the area. They then talk about the physical and emotional challenges they are experiencing. The Social Worker recognises that by helping to address some of this "good life" stuff there will be an opportunity to explore different ways of addressing the physical care support that is also required. The Social Worker discusses the wider and diverse benefits of having a Personal Budget and then agrees a small budget, which the family top up. At this point, because the Social Worker works very closely with the local community and is based in the local high street there is every chance that some connections will be made which will start to re-connect the family back with familiar associations. The Social worker can make a professional judgement at this stage if the family require some additional help to enable them to look creatively at how they use their Personal Budget. This is an investment which will help prevent an escalation of expensive professional input in the future. The creative process will involve identifying all the natural supports which can enhance the overall situation before working on how best to spend the Personal Budget. The Personal Budget could be used for specific "care" or to facilitate this care: Both approaches are more likely to produce better outcomes, be more supportive to the whole family and be more cost effective. The added benefit of this approach is that the more people locally who are involved the more natural the supports are and the likelihood of a growth in local mutual support networks is enhanced: in addition, there becomes a collective learning which will really empower people and build stronger more inventive communities.

I have deliberately not put any labels on any of these approaches because there is a risk of generating a one size fits all approach as soon as you start to categorise, toolkit or systemise any approach. I believe that if we can have some broad goals which recognises the strengths of individuals', communities and professionals, with the flexibility to deliver then all the other pieces will fit together. It's what I would want if confronting similar challenges: It's the spirit of personalisation!

JUST ONE LIFE – Email to a Commissioner

Consequent to our meeting in December...

Dear Commissioner,

When Colin and I met you and your colleagues in December you invited us to contact you directly if circumstances should arise where we felt that the strengths-based, 'support brokerage' approach we practice might achieve much enhanced short and long term benefits.

The package advertised on the Pro Contract System for 17 year old Mr LW seems to us to offer a clear example of the limitations of the needs-based approach that we discussed together. I hope that you share our concerns that, at only 17, this youngster may already be labelled for life as a problem; and experience tells us that, unless he is very fortunate, he will spend most of his life in containing and socially impoverished settings where the potential for neglect and abuse is ever-present.

The Request for Quote specification has a very limited vision that unequivocally ignores the fact that it should be the primary objective of the social care system to work creatively to fundamentally change this young man's life prospects. Instead it states explicitly that, "the overall aim of any service will be to maintain the current positive trend of a significant reduction in aggression/violence."

There is enough in the paperwork that confirms that, had a strengths-based approach been applied to the planning and subsequent iteration of LW's support and development arrangements, a markedly different future is feasible. Relationships, loyalty, and trust are demonstrated as important pre-determinants of socialised behaviour. The need for skilled low arousal and stress reducing support regimes is hinted at but overwhelmed by the weight of concerns about/descriptions of antisocial and dangerous behaviours.

Long experience makes us confident that - by taking the trouble to examine LW's life through a different lens, getting to grips with what really matters to him, addressing life quality as well as behavioural management, working with all the resources and building a strong relationship network, responsively supporting operational staff through the inevitable hard and testing times, and thinking effectively and creatively against the context of a vision of LW's 'good life' – much better and markedly less expensive outcomes are secured.

Would you be willing, given the agreement of LW and his loved ones, to give us the opportunity to demonstrate?

What language are you speaking?

Today, I was invited to a community meeting by a Project worker who was doing a presentation to a number of local community groups around new approaches to obtaining much needed funds. I asked to join the meeting in order to share a little information about some of the work I do locally with families and to talk about the potential for establishing a Timebank in the area.

The first hour of the meeting was taken up by all the participants sharing what they do and why they had come to the meeting. It was really interesting listening to the descriptions of all the different, locally driven, interests, which included a photography group, a drama and multi-arts project for marginalised young people, a local museum, a memory cafe, a community theatre building project, a historic building community centre, and a number of individuals who simply had come as they wanted to contribute in some way to their community. All the Associations were keen to listen to the presenter's ideas about how they could attract new funds, as they were all struggling financially.

The presenter was from a County wide voluntary organisation who had been contracted to "support" local associations and groups in their quest to get "sustainable " funding.

The presentation centred on firstly attempting to define "sustainable funding" and then to categorise the different potential funding streams available to local Associations. I got the strong impression, at an early stage, that the words being spoken were focussing the participant's energies on something that would take them into the world of the "professional" and not build on the obvious strengths of the listeners (the community!). There was a shift away from "community", "relationships" and "reciprocity" to a world of "traded services", "procurement", "tendering" and "business planning" - a shift, which in my opinion, is alien to most of the listeners and definitely did not come across as sustainable for a group of people who were passionate about what matters to their community. The presenter, I think, picked up on this and quickly moved on to finish the session by asking each Association present to fill in a "health check" form which they could return to her at a later date: this would help to focus what **she** needed to do next with each group. It will be interesting to see what happens over the next few months.

It appeared to me that this approach is merely reinforcing the massive gulf between how communities operate and how institutions work. The Associations in that room all operated on the basis of relationships and the goodwill and mutuality (shared passions)of their members. They did not relate or understand (and why should they!) the language of the institution, of business, of a system which still reinforces the status of the "expert" and sadly, they felt compelled to go along (what choice have they got) with the premise that they need to learn the "institutional" language to have any chance of accessing the limited financial resources that may be available to them. It appeared to me that a better approach may of been to listen, trust and then support what is already working well in our communities and not promote "institutional business" approaches as if it were the only show in town.

I then had a few minutes to share a little bit about the work of a couple of people I know who have a learning disability and how they love to contribute in their community: this led me to describe their vision of a community which was able to share and receive skills/gifts and services for the good of each other - a community which was more inclusive, forgiving and safe for all people - a community which valued everybody's contribution towards having a good life . This allowed me then to share a little information about the nature of Timebanking, which was positively received. The meeting ended with an invite to come back to the next meeting, which would start an hour early, to accommodate a more in depth conversation about Timebanking which they recognised as acknowledging the strengths they already have available in their community. I couldn't have asked for more.

Letter to a Policy Maker

Dear Minister,

Citizen Directed Support and Strengths-based Social Care Policy

It was good to see you at Newtown last Thursday. Your energy in maintaining your advocacy for the interests of disabled people and their families, while pursuing other key roles in government, is humbling.

I was the questioner who asked whether, in Wales, we were going to see a government prepared to take a step back; restore real power and autonomy to citizens, their families and communities; and insist that local government and the professions make this a central objective of all social care and community policies?

After more than 4 decades as what might be described as a Social Care professional and, for much of that, leader, and 27 years as the parent of a smashing daughter who has a disability, I am in no doubt that I have lived through an era where institutions and the professions have (and continue to) invaded and occupied
areas of relational and previously communal and reciprocal life with the <u>unintended consequence</u> that families and communities are more dependent, less resourceful, less connected – weaker. The consequences are self evident. Folk are less reciprocal and interdependent and, in many forms, dependent upon consumption. Whether or not consumer society is sustainable is a moot point. What I am clear about is that if we plan the how we care for each other aspects of social policy on the basis of commodified social care the consequences will continue to be institutionalization (we don't need walls), loneliness and isolation, and varying intensities of abuse and neglect.

It was clear from your talk that you associate 'care' overwhelmingly with funded 'services'. We learnt decades ago that services are about tasks and that care is about relationships. When we ask people and those who love them how they want to live with their frailty or disability we invariably find ways to achieve their goals with them that are not wholly and often only minimally dependent upon paid for services. There are many interests that do not want to acknowledge this easily replicable finding. When we ask the many people who feel that no one loves them, we find that their first wish is for help in restoring relationships and belonging. When we (so rarely) have the scope to assist someone to apply their personal budget/direct payment in a free developmental way in pursuit of the life they choose to lead we see far more attention to detail and real accountability than we do in public sector procurement. However people don't often choose the comprehensive – sold in the slave market – products that providers have become accustomed to provide in the economies of scale, dare I say Thatcherite, social market milieu.

Also, in your answer you referred to the imperative of "safeguarding". The term is rolled out habitually in my experience by professionals who are not committed to the central precepts of personalization and not working tenaciously to resolve the real attendant issues, which generally surround accountability for, I prefer to say, community money. Research into what causes us to feel safe and secure demonstrates time and again that most things that Government can do score well down the scale when compared to what family, friends and community can only do in ensuring loving and caring relationships, belonging, social capital and advocacy, real wealth and choice, opportunities to contribute and secure participating citizenship, and so forth. Unfortunately the delivery of needs-defined (defined in terms of what services can do, i.e. tasks) service prescriptions too frequently dilute or actively alienate these natural processes. No matter how often folk demonstrate that if we simply help people get clear about how they want to live with their disability or frailty we invariably evolve patchworks of natural and paid for support that secure better more contributing and integrated lives at significantly lower cost, those with their heads in spread sheets and commercial systems theory, those obsessed with control and quantifiability, those terrified of risk just say, “yes, but”...

And, finally, you challenged us to produce the evidence. I would counter with the challenge that if the only justification for seriously evolving policy is that somewhere else someone has irrefutably proved something, this is prescription for indefensible inertia and, in our case, a counsel for despair that asserts that, despite Nimrod and the AWS, Wales can no longer innovate. It takes a long time for social change to become unchallenged. In Australia it took 20 positive evaluations of Local Area Coordination (a way out of the needs assessment and eligibility ‘trap’) over 23 years before all but one of the States fully implemented the approach and aggrieved professionals and bureaucrats buckled down.

Meanwhile, in the face of the evidence, we continue to tinker with a system that has not much to commend it and looks ever more unsustainable, when more radical directions need, at the least, testing.

In fact, there is a wealth of evidence going back to the 1970’s and probably further. Year on year hundreds of stories of lives enhanced despite obstructive rules and systems are published world-wide– and the list of innovations and innovators who have demonstrated the virtue and efficacy of restoring authority and responsibility to people is seemingly endless. And year on year we run conferences, seminars, events, write reports, even books, set up websites, parade the innovators and thinkers, and strive to bring the evidence to the attention of policy makers. But at a local level professionals reply that this is all well and good but out of step with what government demands while nationally we are told that local authorities and the professions are responsible for the key advice received and acted upon. From a citizen directed perspective we confront a vicious circle!

What we seem a little short of are the political and professional leaders with the gumption, tenacity and longevity to turnaround the oil tanker of needs based and service obsessed policy and practices by getting clear about immutable and far less ambiguous principles, visioning instead of micro-managing, setting objectives and ensuring that they are pursued, and, above all, backing those leaders and practitioners in Wales, of whom there are many more than those known to me, who are striving to work in more strength-based, family/community building and enabling ways.

I and many others want to share the evidence fully and work to demonstrate how the principles can be rolled-in (rather that out) generally. Lots of folk want to demonstrate that people can be trusted to a consistently better job of managing their lives than is achieved under present norms. I am under no misapprehension that, despite the use of the 'right words' in discussion and consultative documents, the notion of really doing it is countervalent. How might we get key players to 'get and think out of their box'?

Yours sincerely,

Bob Rhodes

www.livesthroughfriends.org

The Welfare State

Clement is no longer clement
Nye's spinning berserk in his tomb
Beveridge booms catastrophe's imminent
Their vision careers to its doom

Should these real luminaries arise
Intercede teach and win concessions
From those who institutionalise
And expansionist professions

We'd remember life before the war
By the people for the people our insight
In unison now they would roar
Contribution and more is our right

Unions and mutuals and clubs
The blueprint that drafted our vision
Participation and subs
People governing every decision

Economies of scale are too dear
They reduce us to ciphers and punters
Localism's not a new idea
Been around since the days we were hunters

And gatherers of wealth and power
Will always seek to rule us
Whether through stealth or martial glower
There's some who'll try to fool us

The principle we must defend
And strain to make it focal
Whatever the form we intend
It always must be local

Clues

I'm listening intently for clues to progress
The thought of a good life, it's shining a light
I deal with the pain of a lost decade of anguish
but, the future is bright, they say to agree
the past is a blight, I say, they know that is true
so, we keep track of the pain whilst planning the future
I listen intently for clues to progress
the belief is building, there seems a way forward
but the assessment says this and my family says that
A case for the standing financial committee, they say
A month, a year, my patience is baffling
I listen intently for clues to progress
at last someone confirms the finances
but the strings are relentless, and hope is forgiving
A plan is agreed, but who is it for
All says it getting closer and closer to the door
The fear, the nerves and no recollection
I listen intently for clues to progress
Another year gone, a party for someone
New faces, they ask many more questions
More chat, but what about my weight
There's a place at the back, it's all very cosy
I listen intently for clues to progress

Stay With Me – (song for a good end)

Stay with me
Stay with me
Stay with me while life is passing
Stay with me
Stay with me
Don't want to leave alone

Face the darkness
Strong in trust
Greet the brightness
So you must

Stay with me
Pray with me
Waiting the approaching morning
Lay with me
Say to me
You've never been alone

Ever humble
Always proud
Softly vulnerable
Clumsy loud

Stay with me
Gay with me
Smiling at our shared remembering
OK with me
Your days with me
We've never been alone

Chords
G Em C D7 G Em C D7 G
C Em C Em Am D7 Am D7

Bob Rhodes

Along a Green Way

It's an ancient new dewy May morning
Fresh hedgerows smell green with dazzling briars
Finale of the sloe glow and the dawn of the hawthorn show
He trudges brown booted to his garden
While sparrows and fledgling thrushes trill and thrash
Spritely through tangled shoots and thorns
Fragrance of fresh tilled soil
By the steaming heap where the blackbird delves
To the sty where the warm hogs grumble then delight
Longing for the sweetmeats in his pail

It's another office day in May
And the Weather Man says that it's sunny now
But to take a Mack as it may not stay that way
Though he doesn't mind as he's seldom caught
Between the company car and the office door
Or the Mall or the gymnasium where
He sweats and pants committedly
To exorcise the rigours of the highway
Lacticked by a compromised profession
And lustings of desires for who knows what?

Before he breaks his fast he gilds his hunger in the ramsoned air
Lush banks attend the giggling bouldered brook
Glimpsing a cobalt shooting star eclipse a tiddler from the eddy
His children formed on Sunday of rocks and turves
Imagining that they'd create a carp pool worthy of 'BB' but
Distracted by a Bar-B-Q for tea and ball games in the field behind the shed
That dream awaits another scorching afternoon
He smiles and frees his fowls to the light collects warm eggs
Brown is the brow that wrinkles at the darting wren
That shares the broadcast grain without demur

He knew he'd got the knack the balls knew the score
The way to win identify with winners
Look good be good but not too good
Aspire yourself but endow even more your children who deserving more than you
Must more comply consume achieve unsatisfiable so
Wanting needing seek religion drugs obsessions more possessions
Groomed incapable of sentient reflection

In the mousetrap the hamster's wheel of that eternal rodent strife
Imprisoned customer of every brand even monarchy
Though hovering around a later model to its 1948 conception

Nourished most by the love of those who share his table
Set up for the first part of the day and the chain of ancient hedgerow
He'll lay with art and diligence before as he predicts the weather turns
There's little added just the tools he bears
The billhooks axes raffia's and strings and less is taken away
As all is used or having meagre use consumed by fire
He looks he sees he acts decisively
Cutting straights stakes and stripping lithe heathering
Discerning his pleaches and slicing these with the powerful delicacy
Of a spiritual samurai or medieval continental headsman

He is a good man living for the weekend spend
To taxi praise encourage and so passionately implore
Sweet victories in sports fields dojos dramas or great arts
Vicariously from his two boys he and his love adore
Sunday a fun day to consume to shop to buy to regret
Those things he cannot make grow do perform exchange
Low maintenance gardening Diarmud's hard landscape repelling life
A difference wrought in flooded sub urbanity marsh arid impotent
Bored and hungering for some meaning in the orgy of diversion
Some resolution to the lust for new possession then empty disappointment

In certain worlds those who cannot do die
In every world those who cannot do are prey to those who own -
As Marx's insights much defamed by those with much to lose -
Would declaim the means of production the control of culture
Beliefs ideas and institutionalise knowledge and expertise

Sustain their power secure and occupy man's communal domain
Little or never comprehending that in their domination
Resides their own entrapment and the doom of those
They may never know but love doomed by ignorance
Of essential skills and sweet interdependences for life

Thundering rain abates steams from the gravel track
Across the hillside two brothers amble boots and brogues subtle signatures
He luxuriates in the scents of wet earth herbs conifer and squelch
He is anxious lest another cloudburst breaks ever anxious mopping
He studies the tumbling staccato flittermice gorging siren midge clouds
He skitters pirouettes regretting every splash eyes wide feet alert still splattered
Marvelling absorbed at antics of brown trout aerobatics in the refreshed brook
He loach like alert to all beneath him tender barbuled fearing the eel
Brothers born in nature forged in nurture groomed by chance or choice
I am him and he is me I am me and he is him we are...

Turning Turkey – persuading Commissioners that there can be life after self-direction

We're working on a nut roast Christmas
A vegan answer to our plight
Seeing competition's the road to perdition
Stuffing other poultry just ain't right

We're working on a nut roast Christmas
Making our mark in forestry
No more hard faced vulture in agriculture
Our future role is going to be

We're learning how to poll and coppice
Nurture the cob and almond tree
Never a good reason to doubt the season
Nor waste what nature gives for free

They said turkeys wouldn't vote for Christmas
Forget it please don't moan and groan
Cos we've found a solution that avoids execution
And kills two birds with just one stone

Turkeys were never enfranchised at Christmas
Just served up to the bitter end
When we achieved insight we got a real fright
And saw that change could be our friend

So we're campaigning for a nut roast Christmas
In every freedom we extend
So with principles fit to defend
Please let every turkey be your friend

Dean Poem – A Plea for Self-Determination

There's just a couple of things you need to know about this place
We're a people separate enough to know who's 'them' and who's 'us'
Never paranoid about our vulnerability (cos' it's true!)
To economies of scale in distant halls of power
To those who know the cost but not the price
And never travel up here on the bus

Small was
And could again
Be beautiful here

Reciprocity will as ever meet the bill
When the time comes
As it inevitably will

The disapproval of the clan deals best
With those who unrepentant
Foul the nest

The balm of mutual kindness (not so rare)
Embraces those who've given
And all who fear despair

A life worth living can't be bought
Nor ordered nor coerced with tact
A better future grasped within our hands
Where people care enough to act

Playing Air Guitar

John Etheridge and Richie B weren't born with natural virtuosity
JWT and Machiavelli both learned their special skills intensively

Most public sector folk are all the same
If they don't win they simply change the game
Some steal ideas dilute them from afar
Just playing air guitar

Cos scaling ups the only game in town
They never learn and just dilute things down
Though nothing really changes anywhere
It's not their role to care

People strive hard to swim a yard against the currents of bureaucracy
And when they show the way to go some lazy chancers always copy

Conditioned never to accept the blame
Find lots of fall guys quickly to defame
Don't understand life's different near and far
They're playing air guitar

But worst of all are those who steal your soul
Dilute your efforts loading their bankroll
And never pick a note or hold a bar
They've stolen your guitar

Guest Editor of BBC Radio 4's *Today Programme* – A Fantasy

It's Christmas again. And, as has become traditional, pillars of the establishment (including some safe critics of the status quo) have the freedom to theme the programme for a day; their soapbox to promote their passions, which have a tendency to be for arts and culture, education and science, or a social cause.

I don't, to the best of my knowledge, socialise with media producers. Nor do I have any expectations of occupying any of the elitist pedestals – such as President of the BMA, an Episcopal See, or a 'Booker'. So I don't expect the call to fulfil the role myself.

But I so wish I could! There are so many debates that usually don't or are not permitted to get an airing that one programme won't be enough. Perhaps, after the rapturous reception to my first offering, they might be up for giving me a week every December?

Given the chance, I wonder what I would settle on? There's quite a list of possibilities:

- An exploration of my generation's impact upon and responsibilities towards its successors

- A consideration of sustainable economics from, for a change, the perspective that ethical and sustainable growth is a myth promulgated by the self-interested

- A speculation upon the nature of personal and communal responsibilities and democracy; giving subordinate attention to the advisability of having a non-elected and hereditary person as head of state, head of the established church (theocracy), and commander-in-chief of the armed forces

- A wide deliberation upon the nature of theocratic states in the contemporary world and the impact of faith, mysticism and magical thinking on rational and ethical politics

- A meditation on the subject of social enterprise, including an examination of what the consequences for the concept may be if and when social enterprise becomes a political and institutional strategy

Or...

- Should I stick to my central pre-occupation and start off with a wide-ranging reflection on the nature of 'care' and how we might, in contemporary British society, care for each other through thick and thin?

I don't think that you are likely to find out!

Do the right things!

Despite drumming dictators and dissolute kings
Don't do it right
Do the right things

Paid to do dogma's designed pre-ordainings
Don't do it right
Do the right things

Conformity calms, its opiate balms snoring,
Then one too many an absurd paradox
Keeps me from once more ignoring
That call to free lives from the box

Those who rule and drink their fill
Think they serve a greater cause than us
Who till the earth or drive a bus
Tend our old or serve the ill
They never did and never will

And they know it!

Anger that's spilt
From the denial of guilt
Disgust with self
Like some 'Potterish' elf – sockless!
Clothed, valued, loved and liberated
Incompetence and dependency dissipated
Haloed in earned self respect
No longer groomed to genuflect – reckless?

Need to make sense of everyday things?
Don't do it right
Do the right things

If your life's more subtle than a pile of form-fillings
Don't do it right
Do the right things

Extended Families and Communities – Our Relational Roots?

We came back from an energetic performance of the *African Sanctus* last night and curled up to watch a documentary about frail old age featuring June Brown with our suppers. Her message was bad news for care home entrepreneurs and for the governments they so easily influence. In essence she told us what I believe we all know in our bones. She reminded us that we all, given any choice, yearn to spend our last days of life in our family homes in the bosom of our loved ones.

Then, without delivering the coup de grace that will be my recurring theme, she told us things about which we prefer not to mull. She reflected upon the extended family in which she was raised, the respect and adoration she held for her widowed grandfather who was part her childhood household, and then shared insights into the close extended family relationships that she has nurtured throughout her long life. She, as have so many others, opened the blinds to reveal the loneliness, isolation, vulnerability and often abject emptiness in the lives of frail or disabled people who have fallen out of relationships of all kinds and had this poverty reinforced by dependence upon task oriented services, residential and domiciliary.

Through the lives of friends she once again demonstrated the stoic miseries borne by sole carers for whom, far too often, old age becomes exhausted and ambivalent servitude. Earlier in the evening the *Apprentice* backroom celebrities had, I'm told, been demonstrating that the notion that in the future folk will be expected to work on well in to their seventies is fatuous and ill-founded. But many, many eighty plusses work far harder than any of their lab rats with rarely a rest day or unbroken night! She showed us what a remedial impact is wrought by interactions with family members and especially with children and examples of a lovely local initiative designed to bring a little of this into the lives of the 'institutionalised' but I'd have to say that, inspirational though this was, it was redolent of therapeutic pets, a cuddly diversion rather than a real solution to people's needs for intimate and lifelong relationships and their practical consequences.

So, I'm in no doubt that June is right. The extended family - founded upon love, respect and the interdependency and lifelong contribution of all its members – offers a proven model for how, where the bonds are strong enough, people can care for each other supportively from the cradle to the grave. It provided robust stability for many, perhaps the majority over tens of generations and should be, in my view, regarded as part of a sustainable solution to our current societal crisis. But we must also be respectful of those who are not members of bonded families.

And we must be alert to the fact that the film did not seriously address the reasons for the widespread attenuation of extended families and especially those where three or even four generations cohabit the same property or live within walking distance of each other.

But before I utter the unspeakable (once again) I wish to develop the model a little further and, in doing so, follow June's example and extrapolate from my own experiences.

I grew up in a Gloucestershire village. My mother's family had roots in that community dating back to at least the 15th century. I lived with my parent's and my sister. My maternal grandparents lived in the centre of the village just a few minute's walk away and, in my early childhood, my mum's brother and his family lived at the forge, across the road from my grandparents and abutting my aunt's parent's farm, with the village school across the crossroads from the Non-Conformist chapel that was also central to our lives. My paternal grandparents lived a 20 minute bus ride away and we saw all of these relatives very frequently.

But I don't associate the activities associated with caring and looking out for so much with the personalities amongst my blood relatives as with loved and trusted friends and neighbours. We lived on Church Path, not a metalled road but a narrow, hedged field path that connected our village to the next, bigger one. Medieval farms, crofts, and farm cottages were dotted along our end of the bridle way – a nightmare for deliverers of anything heavy or bulky. Our nearest neighbours were Ida – deaf, loud, jovial school cook who made wine from everything and loved a flutter on the horses – and George and (little) Mrs Cresswell; 'little' because there were two Mrs Cresswell's in the village and the other one was 'big' according to local tradition. It was Mrs C who kept an eye on Mum and me when she had serious kidney problems after my birth. Later in my life, though still at school, I was one of those who sat with George day and night during his final illness. It was Ida, by now retired who kept an eye and fed me while my mother undertook her dinner lady duties at the school during a long recovery from peritonitis and a host of friends and neighbours who had raised my spirits and comforted my parents when they were convinced that I was at death's door. As young as 6 or 7 it was my job, during the cold months, to break the ice on the well at Well Cottage on my way to school so that the old couple who lived there could draw their water more easily. And, after my Grampy's death when I was 7, the lawn and flower beds became my responsibility and that of any mate who chose to help me under my Granny's often critical gaze.

Most of all, on reflection, I'm struck by the intergenerational homogeneity of the time. Whether at work, prayer or play our community did it together. We got a playing field when I was in my teens. Before that Jack Cook's cow pasture was the football pitch in the winter, manicured into the cricket field in the summer. And during the light evenings a crowd of cricketers of all generations would gather, pick up sides and play – with everyone getting a fair crack of the whip at batting and bowling, the youngsters in the process learning give and take and sportsmanship. I suppose I might have been nine or ten when I broke my wrist. Before I bowled off-breaks naturally; after it was looping and dipping wrist spin, leg breaks and googlies. Alec was, to my eyes, a little old man – soon to be retired and not much more that 5 feet in his boots. Probably in his late 50's his son, Derek, was a teenager who was also a part of this 'intergenerational exchange programme'. Alec also bowled leg breaks, high floaters so slow that it was always surprising that they reached and all the more so when you heard the stumps rattle behind you. Wrist spin is a feckless mistress. One day you are unplayable, then for the next week your fielders spend too many grimacing moments retrieving well struck balls from briars, hedgerows and ditches. Alec saw in me a fellow mercurial and misunderstood artist, set out to teach me what he had learned, and took a special interest in my life as a result. He was one of a number, just as I am aware that my parents, through their various interests took a special and guiding interest in the lives of several generations of young friends who, in turn, reciprocated in later life. In this world we knew people warts and all. Respect for elders was not simply a matter of duty or a code; it was a consequence of relationship.

When I look back, my family home was a far from private place. People just called in, meetings were convened around the dining table, teams were selected, jumble sales organised, bible studies conducted, plans hatched and alliances forged. Tea was always on tap and meals for those who opted to partake. People often brought gifts. Flowers or veg from the garden or allotment, cabbage plants wrapt in damp newspaper, something someone had grown out of, a book to lend, a bottle of the latest home brew, or the best of the latest gossip. We reciprocated on our rounds with green string bags of rock cakes (rural ship's biscuit), plums in season, exploding ginger beer, cakes and mysterious preserves. And more, we laboured for each other, lifting spuds, at lambing time, breaking new ground, sharing special skills.

In short, the extended community looked out for just about everyone who had or was contributing to it. That, it seems to me, began to end when big insurance concerns located their headquarters in our vicinity. Houses were built. Our community soon tripled in size. Incomers came – in the main lovely folk but resettled souls who, unthinking, had departed their roots, their extended families and communities in pursuit of career, wealth, and commerce's dangled version of security.

Unwittingly they, and in due order the rest of us, succumbed to the notion that security resides in financial transactions rather than relationships. And it was not long before we came to believe that there is no rational alternative to this perspective. I believe that there is an alternative, a choice that we may adopt as, as I believe it will, our consumer culture declines and falls. It will emerge when our selfish genes wake up to the realisation that our self interest resides in reciprocity and interdependent relationships rather than finding an accommodation with contemporary mammon, the market. It will erupt when we get bored with being distracted and entertained. It will mature as we become more and more indignant about being caste as disposable and manipulable pawns in arrangements that are more the consequence of systems than human coercion. It will blossom when we find the joy and the meaning of life in each other.

And when it is established I've a sneaking suspicion that it will reflect the days of extended families and interdependent and reciprocal local communities and we will return to our roots.

Personalisation - Is it Rocket Science?

My experience, when offered the privilege as a practitioner, of supporting an individual and their family to self-direct has always been positive and is always different. The stories I usually tell are full of complexities associated with challenging a system which "markets" itself as "enabling", "empowering" and 100% behind the commitment to support people to self-direct their own care and to ensure the best outcomes are attained. We all know the reality is somewhat different. As one parent of a young man with learning disabilities told me: "When I stumbled across something called 'personalisation' I thought this would be a chance for me to support me son to fulfil his dream of having his own place, get a job and have a 'normal' life, a life like his older brother. I read the Council's website, which was all about the transformation programme which would offer more choice, empower families, have less bureaucracy, offer individual budgets etc etc. This was the chance my son had been waiting for".

“we are still struggling with
a social care system devoid
of creative intent”

The reality was so different and is probably a story which could be told by hundreds of families across the country. The first years of this initiative delivered extra cash to make it work which you would of thought could of been spent on proving that families and communities can create the real "personal" care required by so many people. However, we all know the reality was a windfall for Local authorities which enabled them to create new "Putting People First" programmes - the only problem was that the people they put first was themselves! That's history, and we are sadly now in a time of austerity with a diminishing financial resource and massive redundancies in the public sector.

The family I am referring to have still not been able to help their son fulfil his dreams and we are still struggling with a social care system devoid of creative intent and a seeming paranoia about letting go of their power. The family's latest feedback was regarding the "resource allocation" which appeared to be offered alongside specific advice about the limits of what the money could be spent on and a statement which advised that the Local authority can no longer support people to live in their own tenancy and group living was the only option being approved by the financial allocation committee. The Social worker also complained that supporting families to have a Personal Budget was so much more complex than "placing" somebody in an existing service. The outcome of this process has been a demoralised family who feel emotionally and physically drained, needing to stop dreaming, about a good life, for their son in order to re-charge their batteries before recommencing battle! How can families be expected to grasp the values of personalisation when they end up battling a system which, on one hand, is promoting and encouraging individuals and families to self-direct, and on the other hand is telling them exactly what they can and can't do alongside an unsustainable increase in bureaucracy and a confused and demoralised professional workforce.

"The outcome of this process has been a demoralised family who feel emotionally and physically drained"

There is a very "simple" way forward, which can utilise existing resources more creatively and start to

build a network of competent and skilled families who can help to move on the "personalisation" agenda without being or feeling punished.
Firstly, the power brokers need to start developing a trusting mindset which commits to breaking down the barriers as and when they are confronted: it is the "Authorities" responsibility to make this happen with all their staff to start building trust with families and communities. This will probably involve a wholesale clear out of procedures and policies which block good practice and contradict personalisation: good leadership, not project officers, will help to ensure there is action in the right places and short termism and protectionism is avoided.
This will involve quite radical reform of front line staff and systems and a ditching of the failed "business" models which have invaded the world of community, society and citizenship over the past three decades. The language of individuals', families and communities has to be used.

“the power brokers need to start developing a trusting mindset”

Secondly, there has to be real, independent (directly accountable) and creative support for individuals and families who want to self direct. Creative thinking is the key skill required when offering this support, not systems thinking. We all now know that when people who require ongoing "care" have strong sustainable Relationship Networks there is a greater chance of experiencing a better quality of life alongside accessing the supports required to address any specific care need. To support someone to have a good life will entail addressing some basic areas fundamental to our personal, physical and emotional wellbeing. This will also have the added effect of enhancing safety and security and enabling

additional choice by virtue of experiencing a more diverse and interdependent life.
A strong Relationship Network will create opportunities to address key components to having a good life: for example, enabling people to have/retain a place to live which they genuinely believe is Home, their refuge, their place of safety, the place people feel most comfortable underpins our individualism; the opportunity to contribute in some way, whether that is through work or other activity is also crucial as we all need to feel like we have something to offer, to contribute. I have, in all my thirty years of practice never genuinely seen a service which really delivers this in the long term: it's always through support of friends and family that will give the continuity required for success. Addressing these area properly is a priority: I'm not one for big lists and form filling or following set procedures as this is the comfort zone of the professional and I know from experience that you are more likely to exclude or marginalise someone if you only go by the book. It has been my experience that when you take this route (whether the individual needs it or not!) and undertake a pre-determined for an assessment or personal plan for everyone you engage with, it is not only a waste of time and therefore resources, but it also disempowers and de-humanises the person you are there to help. It is a fact that action speaks louder than words and people learn when you model what is morally and ethically right for them, at their pace.
It's time we started really moving and believing in this direction (not immediate wholesale change) and as we go, gradually demonstrate the learning by observing the real positive impact on peoples' lives and the changes in the communities we serve. It's not an easy journey or a smooth one, but surely it's the spirit which underpins personalisation and self-directed support. We really do have to stop doing what we have always done: because if we don't, we will only get what we've always got, which, in my opinion, is not good enough.

On the well-intentioned unintended consequences of detailed planning:

'I've spent a lot of my life confused,' I replied. 'You get used to it after a while. There's a lot to be said for merely having a hazy idea of what's going on but generally reaching the right outcome by following broad policy outlines. In fact I've a sneaky suspicion that it's the *only* way of getting things done. Once the horror and unpredictability of unintended consequences get a hold, even the most well intentioned and noblest of plans generally descend to mayhem, confusion and despair.'

With thanks to Jasper Fforde: "The Woman Who Died

Humanize the Beast?

How can we humanize the beast?
The hunting hound hunted hound haunted hound
That snarls between the beast affected least
Saddled far above the quicksand quaking ground
And those who fear that they'll comprise the feast
Who slither dither crane their necks twitch ears
then bound

How can we rid our lives of fear?
The biting snake bitten snake smitten snake
Skulking in dank burrows dark and drear
Secreted behind keypads office glass opaque
Armoured in procedures it's so clear that we're
Too scared to do the right things so we fake

How do we sustain reclaim integrity?
The fighting friend sighted friend never
unrequited friend
Trusting gusting thrusting here there is no paucity
Of evidence that love wins in the end no need to
bend
Our knee to those who cower subverted by the
pedantry
Their fear of life a self afflicted malady that we
can all transcend

How can our beast hold trust tenaciously?
The constant hound sagacious snake foresighted
foxy friend
The certainty that while some will flout our trust
outrageously
And faithless rootless wanderers can by their
waters rarely comprehend
A universal truth that joys outweigh the pain if we
courageously
Commend the worth in all bear disappointments
but don't bend

STOPPING THE ROT OR AM I DREAMING!

Six years ago I parted ways with a medium sized voluntary organisation where I had been a senior Director for over five years. At that time I thought the world would implode and I would become one of these people who went from one job to another retaining some degree of status and pretending to be innovative and caring. I decided on a different route to try and learn what really works for people who require ongoing care and support without having to fight a vested interest by retaining and expanding a large "business" in order to please shareholders or Trustees. I have learnt a lot over the past six years, not all good! It's now "interesting times" - there are massive cuts to social and health budgets and a perceived shift from centralisation to a "localism" agenda. Personalisation continues to be at the centre of how we should be arranging care and individuals are being encouraged to take more control, be more community minded and take more responsibility for their own lives.

It's interesting because, at the same time, I have seen a rise in the number of "think tanks" and "private consultancies" who are peddling their wares on a daily basis, overloading our heads with better ways to do something which could be naturally achieved within our own hearts and minds. The contradictions are out there for all to see and it appears to me that we still have great difficulty letting go of this product called "care" and the insistence that we need "toolkits" to navigate our way through every aspect of our daily lives. It amazes me that for the last decade I and many others have been encouraged to work in a way which empowered the individual to take more control, to think more creatively about their own support requirements and to really connect with community taking personal responsibility for the their own Good Life. I remember experiencing ridicule and violent opposition to anything which undermined the system and power of institutions and professionals. It is now those same institutions and professionals who are pretending to speak the language of "personalisation" and espousing the need to empower communities in order to enable real inclusion of those who are marginalised and re-building a sense of togetherness and care. However, what has happened is the development of a new industry in which these "think tanks" constantly write papers, which state the obvious whilst at the same time imagining that they are eliciting a new way forward whilst creating a new breed of "professional" whose only goal is to create a load of new worthless dependency inducing products to market to a pre-programmed unsuspecting "care customer". I appreciate, having said that, there are clearly a lot of good ideas and approaches that are being described to us which, if used well, could be adapted and used within a UK context. However, my perception is that all these think tanks have taken bits of good practice from around the world and forgot to seamlessly join them all together in the context of the UK, but have focussed on what makes good business to them..

It's probably factual correct to say that there is nothing totally new and no one single approach which is going to be the "one" which delivers great outcomes efficiently and will be the one thing that is going to deliver great care and support to all the vulnerable people in our society. If that was the case then all we would have to do is take what's best from the greatest ideas and deliver the support needed to implement as "best" we can: then adapt and improve to ensure it reflects the specific requirements of the people we work alongside.

As professionals, we have a duty to limit the complexity and respond to individual situations within the context of our society and our community. So, what does this mean? The only way I can relate to this way of thinking is to describe what happens when things go well and then reflect on this learning with the people who really matter (ordinary people in ordinary communities), before taking on board that learning in relation to the next person I work with. No system, policy or process should compromise this approach and any resources allocated should be used creatively in pursuit of the agreed Good Life outcomes, based on the premise that care is something that is freely given between individuals and any supports that are purchased will be complimentary to this approach.

So, how do we stop the rot! Firstly, It is my experience that when you put aside any limiting dogma and open your mind and really listen to what people are saying there are great opportunities to be had and simple but inspiring lives to be had for us all. Yes, this can be done in the context of Local Authority spending cuts, self-directed support, real personal budgets, Asset Based Community Development, Good Life assessing & planning, Local Area Co-ordination etc. But it can't be done by taking any one of these approaches and building a system, a process, a toolkit, a work stream, a traffic light or any other marketable widget. We need to make some big statement which commit us to working differently (embracing all the above), trusting citizens, being transparent (even when getting it wrong!) to generate the different and improved outcomes we all desire. This will mean a genuine equal relationship between public institutions and communities and in the context of a diminishing public purse, a commitment to stripping out the worthless "accountability" departments within our public institutions to ensure the resource we have stays where it is needed. We need to have genuine local Associations at the heart of supporting each other and we need to enable our voluntary sector to do things differently after being told for many years to "act like a business" and respond to the "marketplace", which just doesn't work. There is then a chance to nurture this change and find real innovation which matches our aspiration in the context of an honest appraisal of the available resources. We need to be radical about taking out our rotten core in order to create a blank piece of paper to build what communities really want and to start really caring for one another. Just by taking this first step into the unknown will empower and enable a different vision of what life could be like without the overwhelming pull of the separatist mentality of our consumer culture, or perhaps I am just dreaming!

Colin Campbell

Chant for a Novice Texter

Immortal invisible
What can it be?
Never quite effable
It’s...OMG!

"And the Greatest of These..."

How shall we define describe
The greatest of human qualities
Surpassing faith and love
Or perhaps the most visceral expression
Of the preceding prerequisites
For belonging hugging and forgiveness?

Can we monetize package and sell
Handy bags of faith and love?
Gurus self appointed prophets priests
And mystics pimps courtesans care
Commissioners and Blind Pugh politicians
Ply their glitzy sleazy confidentials - try

Leaving all but the most obsessed
Feeling dirty demeaned deceived
Disappointed disconnected alienated
Sleepwalking into the next salesman's
Transactional solution to
The sad void of the lonely shopper

Is giving alms an act of charity
If it really costs us little in the giving
Leaves us distant unconnected unaffected
Spectators of exotic disasters
Wilfully blind to stresses close to heart and
hearth
That addressed imply true sacrifice?

Is charity just one more human quality
Commodified by the hegemony of greed
Where my reason for existence
Is to consume their stuff?
Should I outsource export my empathy my gifts
Engage in action or transaction?

I felt compelled to compose these verses as yet another seemingly endless 'Children in Need' Telethon started to dominate our TV continuity slots and be referenced in nearly every alleged 'news' (but in reality product placement and promotion) programme. These things make me angry but conflicted. The deal seems to just that, a deal. "Give us your cash for what some might consider entertainment which we will in turn will provide for no fee in return for an opportunity to mimic Savile-style self-promotion and sustain or resurrect our celebrity, earning potential, and chance of a gong. The funds raised will then be passed to a panel of experts who will decide how they will be disbursed. As someone thought it would look democratic to involve the public we have an opportunity to promote ourselves even more through a Big Brother style series of beauty pageant representations of grateful applicants." As I say, I am a little conflicted. Lots of people come together to do heroic and silly things to raise money, often make lasting reciprocal relationships, and as a consequence add to the richness, humanity and resourcefulness of their communities. Lots of important issues that do not get much publicity get some.

The National Lottery (known to many as the 'super tax on the poor' given that wealthy folk tend not to participate) provides another portal for people to hand their cash to another unelected and unrepresentative decider of what constitutes a good cause (that is very susceptible to government's imperatives) in return for a miniscule possibility of becoming absurdly rich. But, while here I am less conflicted, the Lottery does back a lot of innovative initiatives (as well as far too many 'reinventing a broken wheel ones') that would be considered too risky by the public sector unless the proposer was very well connected.

But, viscerally, I worry that we have jettisoned the true meaning of charity and placed it in the alms-giving rather than me-giving card-index of our lives not by choice but because other forces have made it a given that we no longer deem subject to challenge.

Moving the Levers

Looks like I've made it the actress mused
Me and a bishop should I have refused?
On a Question Time Panel with three party hearties
A celebrity feted for going to parties
Giggling and flirting with TV producers
Casting couch venues for public seducers
Who think that the story's the tale that they tell
Who limit the remit and soon ring the bell
If the question that's raised scrapes too close to the bone
Via a patriarch host picked to lift up the tone
Show folk that our betters always know best
With wisdom and knowledge denied to the rest
With wisdom and knowledge obscured by deceit
From everyone bar the insider elite
That colludes exploits the paradox
Outsider hen insider fox

You're everything to me – so suffer and shrink

Impassioned the crooner's drooling obsession
Comprehensive no room for concession
I'll be your everything sung with intent
Hell will ensue if he doesn't relent
He'll be your gaoler your owner your muse
You're gaining so much don't fear what you'll lose
Romance reigns for moments real love a lifetime
Wide trusting unsabotaged by a rhyme

Tip top professional expert and caring
Award winning systems numb to the swearing
Of customers born demanding dependent
On firms ever spinning process resplendent
Transparent images formed through a prism
Skilled self-deceivers who to avoid schism
Devalue language dull meaning and thought
Deluded pretend that true love can be bought

Impassioned the Minister's eager to please
Simply relax and hand over the fees
Being our hero that's his intent
Hell has ensued as he didn't relent
Persuasive plausible attenuator
Of families friends the community traitor
Profits rank services tasks by the pound
Grinding life's essences into the ground

Man undervalued just suffers and shrinks
State overblown corrupts till it stinks
Possession implies a lifetime in chains
Leave it to us lord of toxic refrains
We is the mantra of those who succeed
We the solution in every creed
Us bold grandchildren of creativity
Strong and secure in a culture of we

You Can't Place Me! (I may be indisposed, but I'm not ripe for disposal!)

Not now, after a lifetime of giving, sharing, and caring,
Now that the often inevitable has come to pass
Now I've just a little to give and official faces of pity mouth "vulnerable",
Insist and take me at risk to their self anointed power
Ignorant of, excluding those who know me and would take a different view
My silent voice screams, you can't place me!

Of course you can't place me. You don't know me;
The comings and goings of my life, how the world touched me and I stroked it.
But I can place you. I've watched, attended your offices and discussions,
Read your justifications, been dismissed as some romantic fool
As your mission of humanity has been redefined as a matter of economy
And love prostituted to career. I can place you!

So, in my vulnerable time, don't use that word!
You know, that placement word that redefines me as a transaction, a price, jobs and growth!
The grave is a placement, the finality of fire, no different inertia to the lingering of disconnection
Except that pain persists. Life is messy, no matter that you pissed yourself laughing or crying.
Our story, our history a litany of acts, omissions, connections, credits and debts is formed
Of complex blood, brain, and sinew, lifelong relationships.
So don't place me. Reconnect me!

We Don't Like Democracy

We don't like democracy
It just gets in the way
Of letting them do what they'll do
While we work (if we're lucky) and play

It seems there are unwritten rules
Unspoken and arcane
That circumscribe their powers to do
What financiers ordain

There doesn't seem a lot of point
We don't need to enlarge
It's obvious to one and all
Our power's (theirs included) just a mirage

They can fiddle at the edges
Orchestrate to get elected
Conduct dramatic overtures
But they're easily rejected

If dystopians inform their tongue
Or their thinking flutters free
Forget that those who used their vote
Aren't their constituency

But they are sadly symptoms
We are equally to blame
Because we are such patsies
To a coercive game

We're such suckers for a circus
To celebrity we clamour
We're groomed and tuned from early years
To forelock tip to glamour

We're phlegmatic balanced British
Tolerant of contradiction
But it could be said in our case
Tolerance is an addiction

Much maligned Karl Marx observed
Religions quieten indignation
In our consumer dreamlike state
Entertainment breeds stagnation

It seems that we're content to play
A pawnish role at best
Disempowered disposable
A baby at the breast

We're Peter Pans weak childish fawns
Never seeking to make sense
If at the ending of our lives
We've made no difference

We'll shop covet acquire more debt
Diversion's church attend
Cheer for a queen swoon for a star
Blame incomers drive a 3 litre car
Bank on science to extend lives
To play online games when we're 95's
Look for meaning in superstition
Look for meaning in television
Look for meaning in diversion
Find some solace in perversion
Look for meaning in career
No-one's indispensible here
Find that if all's loose no tight
Relationships won't work out right

With the smooth comes the rough
Some times in life are always tough
At these junctures we need time
To give and take to sing to rhyme

(To address human needs, belonging loving, caring, giving, growing, sharing, nurturing without risk to our wealth (real meaning), employment/income – maybe I don't want business to pay taxes – perhaps instead I want them to contribute to society by giving their employees all the time they need to be fully human, fully interdependent, reciprocal, affirming, engaged with and responsible for kith & kin)

Democracy? We'll admit it's got its uses?

June 27, 2008

Who's with "Homo Mimicus"

From Eric Zapetal

I propose a hypothesis, summed up by changing our name from Homo sapiens, "wise man" to Homo mimicus, "mimicking man". Many animals mimic each other's behaviour but we do it more often and with greater fidelity. Our compulsive copying encodes collective knowledge into our society, and it is really our society that possesses humanity's "intelligence".

Consider two islands, identical except that one has a population of highly intelligent but vain apes, while the other has a population of gregarious dimwits that love mimicking each others' actions.

The "sapiens" are always inventing marvellous gadgets but their vanity is such that they will never use another's clever idea.

It is only by accident that a dimwit discovers that poking a honey-coated stick into a hollow log will pull out some delicious termites. But, seeing this many mimicus copy it. Some of the copied actions improve the chances of survival of the sub-population performing them.

Which species is most likely to develop megacities or rocket ships? I'd back the dimwits.

A Biblical Parody

THE LORD THY EXPERT IS A JEALOUS EXPERT THOU SHALT HAVE NO OTHER EXPERT BUT ME!

Do we ever consider the motivations of those who claim expertise?

THE QUESTION

What might we possibly do in order to create both the time and will within our society to care for each other?

Confused or Conned.com

Choice is good shouts liberty
Choice and fairness on our lips
Every time we pose to speak
Choice the essence we decree
Squeeze the point to squeaking pips
Consumerist democracy serves the strong exploits the weak
Or did I somehow get that wrong?
Check at confused or conned.com

Was it choice that caused so many
To laud their born subordination
Dismiss their craven subject ranks
And for not even one bright penny
Be traitors to a democratic nation
With no shells loosed from monarch's tanks?
Or did I somehow get that wrong?
Check at confused or conned.com

Was it choice that caused our young
In classrooms up and down the land
Curricular instructions waived
In faltering voices to give tongue
In martial lines to loyally stand
For her the song said must be saved?
Or did I somehow get that wrong?
Check at confused or conned.com

Did we choose the media hacks
Demand their suave sophistications
Their rabble rousing propaganda
They glamorize avoid brass tacks
Pen sanctimonious perorations
Ignore the jewels from Dr Banda
Or did I somehow get it wrong?
Check at confused or conned.com

I wonder if there is in France
A presidential correspondent
It would be strange if there were not
Because in France there's quite a chance
He could do something quite important
While monarchs can't decide a lot?
Or did I somehow get that wrong?
Check at confused or conned.com

And have our friends in France and Eire
More savoir faire than Anglo-Celts
As leading commentators here
Abjure the thoughts of President Blair
With knob on tongue that never melts
Unblushingly imply that we're too gullible to
choose well my dear?
Or did I somehow get that wrong?
Check at confused or conned.com

There's something in us of the herd
A drive that says we must belong
While those of us who won't be groomed
Who echoes sense of Nuremberg
Who stand out boldly from the throng
Are mocked or feared shut out or doomed
Or did I somehow get that wrong?
Check at confused or conned.com

The monarchy a British brand
That's wrapped itself in patriot's gear
Like pippins, beef and fish and chips
Asserts "We're worth it" watch rock bands
Strut on our roof while the old dear
Does her duty rarely slips
Or did I somehow get that wrong?
Check at confused or conned.com

Commerce knows the lure of choice
Pluggers glory in its power
Substituting if with what
Hearing no dissenting voice
Letting no opponents flower
Groomed before we quit our cot
Fitting in we can rejoice
One of masses in our tower
Deluded pawns consuming rot
Little know we now of choice

Organ grinders have the power
Oft stroked monkeys just do not
Or have I somehow got it wrong?
Check at confused or conned.com

Bring in the Pseud (Living to Give)

Isn't it strange?
Is it a joke?
Making books bingo games
Lifelong jobs for most folk?
Importing food
Bring in the pseud

Everything shouts
You should work to be
A presenter or gormless celeb
On the TV
Can't mend a plug
Salute the mug

We've been adroit
Quick to exploit
All the margins and assets that lurk
Between others' work
Now we've been rumbled
Profits have tumbled
As we thrash about in the poo
We haven't a clue

Don't you rate crafts?
Manufacture?
Harvesting wind and tapping the waves
Agriculture?
Time for your kin
Secure in your skin

Disregard those
Who rule and direct
Who bluster and cluster and pose
But never connect
Stuck on their wheel
Immured from the real
Whose power is lent
To the rich and the bent

Is there a chance?
Could it just be
That we'll choose sustainable lives
Before tragedy?
Rid of our lice
No longer mice?
Working to live
Living to give!

“...if people do not have responsibility,
do not expect them to behave responsibly.”

Carne Ross – The Leaderless Revolution

Meeting of Minds and the Elephant in the Room

Part of my day to day work involves working alongside families, supporting them to co- ordinate the support and care of a family member. This role is often called Support Brokerage but I'm increasinglyseeing people calling themselves “Support Brokers” without really knowing what this means – but that’s another story!

“families have often been labelled by professionals as a “problem” or “difficult” when all they want is the best for their loved one”

The role involves working alongside the person who requires the additional support while enabling some planning before helping with the plan’s implementation. In some ways this is the easy part as I’m usually working with people who have experienced poor support in the past and have been very frustrated with the system they have encountered and therefore ready for change. Sadly, in my experience, these families have often been la- belled by professionals as a “problem” or “difficult” when all they want is the best for their loved one.

What I want to describe is a recent review I attended which was convened by the Independent Living Fund in relation to an individual I was supporting. The review had been convened because the person I was supporting (& his family) had, 18 months previously, decided that they were fed up with the way "care" agencies had been supporting them over the past 3 years and wanted to implement their plan in a more creative way in order to get the outcomes they really, really wanted. At the time they made this decision the main funding body (the Local Authority) had been quite dismissive of the family's ability to use the funds allocated to them (Personal Budget) in a way that could facilitate the 24 hour "care" required to sustain an individual tenancy arrangement. This was because the original funding was allocated on the basis of three people sharing a house with a high element of shared support. Fundamentally, the Local Authority didn't believe this could be achieved based on the resources (money) they had allocated to this individual's Personal Budget and they clearly indicated there would be no more money forthcoming. At the time we did discuss the consequences of asking for more money but decided there was enough in the budget to deliver our agreed plan. Since making that decision, the life of the person who requires care has greatly improved and he is now living in his own tenancy supported by a mixture of directly paid supporters, family and friends. His assessed need for overnight care/support is addressed by having a Homesharer who offers some help in exchange for free accommodation in a nice house. When no Homesharer is available, which can happen when one Homesharer leaves before another one is recruited, he receives support from his own staff and family when needed: no agencies are involved, which means the staff have increased pay, which fairly reflects the work they do, and the overall cost is lower. This flexible arrangement has led to greater opportunities for the person being cared for to con- tribute locally, an expanding relationship network, a healthy lifestyle and a more relaxed and "in-control" family. The overall costs also reduced significantly (15-20%) which is why the Independent Living Fund requested a review, because it's not often that people want to hand money back!

"overall costs also reduced Significantly"

The review day came and we all sat down in the lounge over a cup of coffee. The meeting was attended by me, the individual who was receiving money from the Independent Living Fund, his Personal Assistant, his parents, the Independent Living Fund assessor and a representative from the Local Authority Finance Assessor. The meeting started with a general feedback around the achievements of the past 18 months since all agencies were dropped and a more creative and inclusive approach was taken. The list was impressive and the main points are illustrated opposite. Overall, it had been a good 18 months with lots of positives and a real sense of “this is what life’s all about”, and most importantly a sense from all parties that control had been regained and there was now a real opportunity to have sustainable control in order to deal with everything that life throws up!

<u>My Good Life over the past 18 months</u>

☺Moved into own tenancy

☺First 12 months had a Homesharer

☺Started own micro-business after successfully obtaining a grant from UnLtd

☺Became part of the local Britain in Bloom Association

☺Started taking responsibility for maintaining a piece of public space which was in disrepair

☺Increased my circle of friends

☺Feeling a lot safer after problems in the past

☺Going to the gym on a regular basis

☺Improved health (emotional & physical)

☺Have friends visit overnight

☺Arrange barbeques and “socials” when I choose

☺Spending some time by myself (with arms- length support)

☺Feel my house is now my “home”.

☺Am more relaxed, especially when interviewing.

☺Stopped going to the same college courses

☺Parents are less stressed

☺Less contact with Social Work Department

☺Helped organise and deliver a local “high street” community consultation day

☺Taking part in establishing a local TimeBank

All agreed - hooray! However, there was a challenge around how the Independent Living Fund could record this on their forms because every week the support was different and the Local Authority rules and the Independent Living Fund rules didn't match! At this point my heart sank as I had been in this situation before. I've had many conversations with Local Authorities who find it difficult when families use their Personal Budget creatively, even though the outcomes are better than the traditional route. It is also sometimes problematic for Local Authorities to take money back if someone under-spends without punishing them the next year. But this time there appeared to be a meeting of minds and the representatives from the Independent Living Fund and the Local Authority Finance department got together (in a huddle) and agreed they would take personal responsibility for making sure there were no issues arising because we couldn't fill in the right boxes on their forms and they would make sure we complied with all the contradictory regulations that central and local governments have.

"this way saves money, reduces stress and will have minimal impact on the person who happens to have a support need"

There was also a commitment to not reducing the budget for next year as they realised that we would only use what was needed and the rest would be returned next year if there was an under-spend. I also like to think they realised that, by not reducing the budget, we could deal with any crisis that comes up and blips in support requirements over the next 12 months without having to go back to the referral system and try to get additional funds which would take up a lot of time from professionals and administrators. This way saves money, reduces stress and will have minimal impact on the person who happens to have a support need: all he wants is a Good Life with minimal interference from professionals. After the meeting I had some feedback from the Local Authority representative who said "It was good to see you today & I was really impressed with the care package that is now in place. I have known the family for many years and have to say that the current mobility, well-being and general happiness is up there with the best that I have seen of him.

I'm sure that there are other people who could benefit from the personalised care & support & that the Local Authority would appreciate the savings made.
It's worth highlighting that if the people in that meeting had been driven by systems, policies and procedures, I think there would have been a totally different outcome that would of undermined all the hard work, trust and learning achieved over the previous 18 months.

How many individuals and families do you know would feel confident about accessing a Personal Budget knowing there is only, at best, time limited support and how many would be as creative as this family? The fact is, we now appear to be viewing Personal Budgets as something which has to be rolled out in order to "tick the boxes" of the personalisation agenda and to do this we are adopting a one size fits all approach based on outdated policies and procedures that reflect what we have always done and not what we want to do.

If we really want to implement personalisation in order to make a positive difference to the thousands of people who require additional support, and we know the current system of care is not sustainable, we have to acknowledge the elephant in the room. Adults and children (who require care) and their families cannot be expected to implement a policy that most professionals don't understand and is written in the language of institutions and not of communities which, when I last looked, is where most people live.

Colin Campbell

In any language (a bit of fun) the medium is relationships...

Fortitudo in Paradoxum

Walking the dogs in a dank dawn as the year turned
I passed, as I often do, the old forge and glimpsed in recollection
The coke and smoked-smeared craftsman toiling in the fire
Smelt the reddening iron, combusting primordial life, the rust
Setting teeth on edge as his anvil rang announcing the daily mystery
The alchemy of fire and force, quenching water, tempering heat,
Of sweat and skill, tenacity and love, intellect and feel, the intuition
That melds the brittle with the soft, the fibrous with the hard
A metaphor for our enigmatic state, a paean of perplexity
Ineffable complexity and ultimate simplicity.

Bywyd yn ffurf ar gelfyddyd

Learned from the valley's smith while the children
Wide-eyed senses leaping, alert and eager in the iron spit smoke
Wielded gnarled old rusted hammers in awe of the ancient magi
Calloused swathed in holey leather, pincers holding tightly
The tiny horseshoes to be borne home and nailed above the door
And the souls of those who heard that when you're burned
The working blacksmith's fortune lies in holding
The hurt close to the fire, as near as draws tears to any hero's eye,
This being as magical as his gravely given injunction to pin their charms the right way up
His power the sonar of his tone, to them great age, the knowing twinkle of his eye.

Partager et prosperer – Elaa hyvin anna

I'm Kevin Coyd a drummer
From rainy Cefn Coed y Cymer
No one local thought me barmy

To do my drumming in the army
Cos there's no work here in Cymer
In Cymer that's where mam and pa
And brothers Matt and Hywel are
And buxom Mab who really cared
But left her feelings undeclared
Who, three kids on, lives with her ma
There isn't much enjoyment
In windswept chronic unemployment
I shut the thought out of my head
That soldiers often come home dead
Until my first Helmand deployment
When I felt the stress of doing
What the great bite off but leave their servants chewing
The gestures soaked in children's blood
Of putrid flesh in quaking mud
Paranoia justly brewing; forgive them? They know what they're doing!
We're here they said to make the people free
To liberate the victims of a tide of zealotry
But soon I feared and loathed them every one
Each gift a bomb, each war worn face a gun
What would I do if I was forced on me?
If turbaned bands of squaddies sashayed in my street
Clearly never sure if friend or foe they'll meet
I'd want them gone, I'd want them out
This invasion, this occupation is far more about
Defence of privilege, of wealth, and keeping arms purveyors sweet
And in a flash I saw the reason for this war
How men-at-arms and international law
Protect and promote the source of desperation
That drives the hopeless poor to seek salvation
In tribal dogmas and faith's never reasoned roar
So now I'm back in cloudy Cymer
Limbs intact but I'm a hummer
Who shuts thoughts out of my head
And wishes that I'd come home dead
Or never been that soldier drummer
Who's in a purgatory of confusion
Self loathing at his cavalier collusion
With that revenge-fired insincerity,
The powerful crazed with their posterity,
Inured to the stinking truth of their delusion
(promulgated as they disregard the different and distant as disposable, not valued, not valid.)

Invalid Kevin in his home town
Ex-soldier with a chiselled frown
Exposing the invalidity of those
Who sanctified in martial clothes
Funeral march around our town
Divest your arms, invest in Cymer,
A future for our hopeless drummer
And for so many more to come
So they can march to their own drum
Turn Cymer's sadness into summer
Support the strength, the love and care
That succours Kevin now he's there
His family, friends, and steadfast Mab
Declares for Kevin as her children's Dad
Belonging is the grist they share
As come what will they're always there.

Condutor on Pascexeiro? Escolle

They say that they will make it better
They'll limit what we have to pay
For what we never really wanted
To an amount that most of us can take foregranted
When our time comes to benefit
We'll be already ash or clay
And most of us who bought our castles
In capital's democracy
Maggie's self-sufficient loyal swarming masses
In the ditch like Third World asses
Tsetse'd patsied by that doxy
Our sweat their sublime hypocrisy
Workers drones quite dispensable
To a system undisputed
Shadow elite beyond the reach
Of those who legislate investigate impeach
Of those who'd live another way
And find their culture foul polluted
Protected by pervasive myths
Of choice and opportunity
The circuses of classic times and Latin dogmas of the past
Marx's opiates redefined and massed
In betting bingo bands the boxed obsessions sex and sport
The new redeemer omnipresent fawning slick celebrity
So now they can't afford the market
That they inspired as honest trade
And now we've been detached deskilled
Vulnerable needy shoppers unfulfilled
Plausible insurers in their stables will orchestrate the next illusion
Will spring the pre-planned traps that have been laid
To redistribute the wealth of millions
From the many to the few
To the authors of our culture
Loach hyena maggot vulture
Timeless masters of the chaos makers of the bedlam...
...Unless we choose to fuck them up
By opting out by not conforming

By associating conspiring seeing solutions in solidarity
In interdependence with the many like ourselves
Attending to our friendships loyalties and ties that bind
Us to each other as sappers in bomb-craters
Mums when a little one is lost and neighbours with a threat a cause
Marrow deep the antediluvian drive to seek survival and renewal only through each other
Without a script sans forms unpatterned
Given shape by love's integrity
By the joy of being needed

Bob Rhodes

Have I the right?

I must confess to often being in a quandary about my locus or justification for speaking out so bluntly and often angrily about the iniquities and absurdities that I perceive in contemporary 'social care' arrangements and the general superficiality and disconnectedness that, for me, characterizes a social economy that is too much in tow to money.

I'm presently reading Christopher Hitchens' memoir, *Hitch 22*, and found a little comfort in his rationale for the nature of his involvement with the "hard" left in the 60's:

"...we earned our claim to speak and intervene by right of experience and sacrifice and work. It would never have done for any of us to stand up and say that our sex or sexuality or pigmentation or disability were qualifications in themselves."

A smack in the teeth for the fetish of political correctness and self-interested consumerism, don't you think?

Have I the right to scold you?
You know I've always told you
We need each other at the core.
Have I the right to ruffle
Agitate and cause a scuffle?
Get labelled as a crashing bore?

Have I the right to reflect
Draw conclusions not be suspect
When my solution's not the norm?
Have I the right to innovate?
Those with power will always frustrate
Those who see beyond and can't conform

It's in our genes
We just can't bear it
When our future's at risk
We have to share it
There's a far better life
When we all belong

I have the right to model
Better options than the twaddle
Bodged up by our systematic tinkers
I have the right to question
Make the radical suggestion
That we all remove our blinkers

I have the right of learning
To share the insights that are burning
Undimming through reflective nights
The responsibility of one who's struggled
Innovated iterated studied and juggled
Refining meanings beyond rights

Bob Rhodes

Into the darkness of light

Their smiles may be for me,
the lady's who took me in her arms
and the man's who held my mother's tight.
They are warped by my tears
like the soft colours of the bedroom
they say is mine.
The policeman has gone
and I am alone
for that they have bathed away the smell of me.
This place is not home,
but a place, they say, of safety,
the start of a new life
without pain or danger.
Its strangeness fills me with fear.

Ken Davies 2010

Into care

I tremble fearful, tearful, blind
to smiles that seek to comfort me;
the life I knew is left behind,
the one to come I've yet to see.
The pastel coloured walls that close
the light of day from my sad eyes
enfold me as the darkness grows;
within their safety my heart cries.
I do not know these clothes I wear;
their warming comfort cannot heal
the frozen scars and dank despair
that cause the coldness that I feel.
I only know these skies so grey,
For me the way it's always been.
I search it for the breaking day
I cannot know, not having seen.

Ken Davies 2010

The Blood Myth

"I'll tell you what", the Leader said, sprawled on a pink settee,
"If it's as good as the words you weave you certainly won't need me.
And that's as well as our strong belief, applied to innovation,
Is that anything can be marketized and not need a state donation.
So take your bold ideas for change, of love and equity,
And package them in ways that will appeal to folk who think like me.
Play down the social benefits, scale up the dividends,
And soon you'll find in halls of power you've many happy friends.
Focus on great savings, that shrink establishment,
Grow electronic systems, end recalcitrant mismanagement
Serried banks of keypads and worried ranks of ciphers
Following procedures like chemically castrated lifers.
Glamorize your offer", he lectured on, "stress its exclusivity
To those with strength, acuity - in other words, like me.
The market's the solution, there's gold in them there Bills",
He chuckled, dismissing the misanthropy that his approach distils.

In former times priestly elites to forestay drought and flood
Deluded rulers with one cure, the sacrifice of blood,
So ignorant and bestial, vainglorious deceivers
Betrayed, debased, devalorized those innocent believers
In whose potency and graft the true potential lay
But for their status, wealth and power they led their flock astray
And made them suffer grievously, kneel neath the myth that pain

Redeems, protects and sanctifies the loved ones that remain.
Exploiters who dare not concede the failure of their lore
Exceeded deaths from famine in grim ecstasies of gore
Are redolent of ealdormen endowed with current sway
Who, fearful of unmasking, assert that there is no other way.
No other way to serve their creed, keep toilers in their place,
Hang onto power, stay out of gaol, and most of all, save face.
May be, as in ancient times (and wild places ever),
As myths explode and elites implode, it's our time to endeavour.

So be ready!

INDEX

Welcome to my take on an absurd World 1
Bridging the Rubicon 4
Can life be simply branded as commodities? 9
Doing the Right Thing 13
A Public Health Model of Social Care Regulation? 17
They will not control us – we will be victorious? 24
On the Care Market – A Parody 28
A Daft Idea? 30
Let's vote Rikki Semler for President 37
A Lesson from the Lottery 38
A Strategy for Self-Direction 45
On Leadership 48
It's the Toughest of Commissions 50
Simple Lessons from the U3A 52
Sitting with George 55
A Place for Rose 58
I'm Ray – an expert on institutions 61
Dreaming of a Life without Professionals 66
Little Loner 70
Making Comets of Little Stars 71
When Nothing is Your Meaning 75
Billie Placement (1) 79
Billie Placement (2) 84
Reviewing Your Good Life 88
Getting Rhys to School + Tinker Tinker 92
What Goes Round 96
Systems in Action 100
Just One Life – email to a Commissioner 104
What Language Are You Speaking? 106
Letter to a Policy Maker 109
The Welfare State 113
Clues 114
Stay With Me – A Song for a Good End 115
Along a Green way 116
Turning Turkey 119
Dean Poem 120
Playing Air Guitar 121
Guest Editor of Radio 4's *Today Programme* – A Fantasy 122
Do the Right Things! 124
Our Extended Families and Communities – Our Relational Roots 125
Personalisation – Is it Rocket Science? 130

On the Well-Intentioned, Unintended Consequences of Detailed Planning 134
Humanize the Beast? 135
Stopping the Rot – or am I Dreaming? 136
Chant for a Novice Texter 140
"And the Greatest of These..." 141
Moving the Levers 143
You're everything to me – so suffer and shrink 144
You Can't Place Me! 145
We Don't Like Democracy 146
Who's with Homo Mimicus? 148
A Biblical Parody 150
The Question 151
Confused or Conned.com 152
Bring in the Pseud (Living to Give) 154
A Quote From Carne Ross 155
A Meeting of Minds and The Elephant in the Room 156
In any language (a bit of fun) the medium is relationships... 162
Have I the Right? 167
Into the Darkness of Light 169
Into Care 169
The Blood Myth 170

"A poet's work is to name the unnameable, to point at frauds, to take sides, to start arguments, shape the world and stop it from going to sleep."

- Baal the poet in "The Satanic Verses" by Salman Rushdie

ND - #0100 - 080726 - C0 - 156/234/10 - PB - 9781780356037 - Gloss Lamination